Go Ask The Dead

BY **FRANK TROPEA**

Go Ask The Dead

THE TALE OF A GIRL IN A HAUNTED LAND OF CIVIL WAR AND SLAVERY

ReadersMagnet, LLC

Published in the United States of America
ISBN Paperback: 978-1-950947-07-2
ISBN Hardback: 978-1-949981-61-2
ISBN eBook: 978-1-949981-62-9

This is a work of fiction. Names, characters, places and incidents either are the product of the author's imagination or are used fictitiously, and any resemblance to any actual persons, living or dead, events, or locales is entirely coincidental.

The opinions expressed by the author are not necessarily those of ReadersMagnet, LLC.

ReadersMagnet, LLC
10620 Treena Street, Suite 230 | San Diego, California, 92131 USA
1.619. 354. 2643 | www.readersmagnet.com

Cover design by Ericka Walker
Interior design by Shemaryl Evans

Fifteen-year-old Mandy Mannon put some red lipstick on her perfect cupid bow lips. She had already put on a little of her mother's makeup upon her face. Looking at herself in her mother's large shining mirror, she looked at her reflection and smiled. Her hair was long and golden like her mother's, her missing mother Aurelia's hair. Her mother had been missing now for several months. But when she had suddenly gone missing one early November dark night, like a bright penny falling into a gutter, Amanda, or Mandy as she was called about her house, hadn't cried at all.

Aurelia hadn't really been much of a mother to her. While not being physically abusive to her, just very emotionally neglectful. It was Delia, the black cook and general maid, who had gotten her up and dressed and fed and off to school. Her lovely mother had her other concerns. At ten, Mandy had suddenly realized that her mother had secret assignations with men. Why, before she'd married Ted, her stepfather, her mother had brought her lovers home to the small luxurious mansion that was her home.

They were mostly young, rough, strong-looking men in workmen's clothes. Sometimes at night, Mandy would hear the raucous sounds of her mother's lovemaking of one of several or, indeed, all at once of several of men she'd brought to her bedroom. Sometimes, her mother giggled like a school girl with her lovers. Aurelia had never told Mandy just who her father was. When she was twelve, Mandy suddenly realized that from the way her mother behaved and cavorted with her young men, she herself did not know who her father was. When she was thirteen, she suddenly thought, *Oh, why did it all matter anyway?* Her mother's sudden marriage to Ted Basker three years ago had surprised Mandy. Ted was a handsome corporate lawyer. Like her mother, with her Devereaux blood, he had come from money.

He really seemed to like Mandy, and she loved him in turn. After her mother had married Ted, her errant lovers had not come anywhere to the house. But her mother, as if compelled by the fire consuming her, had still stayed out late nights when Ted was busy in his study on his million-dollar cases. Mandy knew her mother was enjoying her lovers at night secretly—or not so secretly as her classmates, boys and girls at the Cheswick Private School in the area, had openly mocked and derided her for having such a wanton, a trollop for a mother.

At night sometimes when Aurelia was home, Mandy could hear her mother and Ted fighting mercilessly about her so open affairs. To her, it was pointless, cruel really—that was just how her mother was. It was her way. Why, to argue and harangue her mother for her immoral ways was like yelling at a female cat for going so repeatedly and openly into heat.

And come to think of it, no one had ever told her, Mandy, the precious facts of life. But she had kind of figured that out on her own when she was eleven or so. As she basically knew, with her newly budding alabaster and pink breasts, that the boys in her school were beginning to look at her longingly. She knew what that was about. Not that she had any friends at school, but the boys were gazing at her rather heatedly. Even Ted, in the newly empty mansion was looking at her with a new interest. In fact, yesterday he had asked her to use her mother's makeup, dress up in her best gown and have a wonderful dinner with him of beef Wellington and vegetables Southern style.

Delia had been ordered to cook her very best and to bring the bottles of vintage wine out.

Delia had looked startled and then suspicious but, like a soldier taking orders, had obeyed. Ted had also given her an extra $100 and gave her the night off after she had cooked the delectable dinner and set the table with the finest white, creamy tablecloth and sterling silverware. Before she had left for her home in the slum Bourbonville, she had gotten Mandy in a corner of her bedroom and told her to be careful tonight for she would be all alone with her stepfather, "I don't want you to behave like your vanished mother, girl. You all be good now. God Himself is looking down on you tonight and you is almost a woman now. Be good, hon, I love ya."

Amanda was embarrassed but also grateful for Delia's concern. If only her missing mother had shown even half of Delia's care, love, and concern, but that had never happened.

The dinner with Ted went very well. He had specially dressed for this dinner in a wonderful dark lawyer's suit. Though it was a bit big and loose on her, at Ted's ringing urging, Mandy had dressed in one of her missing mother's most lovely crinoline and silk white gown. Her mother had looked like a stunning fashion model in it. Mandy, to please Ted, had even sprayed on some of her mother's very expensive, flowery perfume too.

Ted complimented Mandy profusely and looked at her a bit heatedly. Ted looked so, so devastatingly handsome with his black, black hair and blue, blue eyes with the rugged, handsomest features she'd ever seen on any man. He'd played some football in college and had a nice, rugged build too.

Briefly, in a lost little girl fashion, she wondered to herself how could her vanished mother have ever been unfaithful to him? When she was a grown woman, if she had as handsome a husband, she'd never be unfaithful at all. But then Ted said that she would grow up to be even more beautiful than her mother, Aurelia, and Aurelia, whatever her terrible faults, had been very beautiful indeed.

The compliment made her blush rose red. Then Ted poured her a glass of special Bordeaux wine, though she had never drank alcohol before. She was only fifteen after all. But to please him and to satisfy her own curiosity, she drank some of the deep red wine. She accidentally gulped it down naturally. It stung her mouth a little, but she did not find the sharp taste unpleasant. After she had drunk it all, Ted poured her another, and she drank it more slowly this time.

Soon, she felt light and silly and a little as if she were floating. When Ted said how really beautiful she was again, she said to him, "What a complete fool my mother is or was. I don't know after all if she's still alive or dead. But she's a fool, a silly asinine fool."

"Why do you think that, Mandy?" he asked, smiling so handsomely at her.

"Because if I had a husband as handsome as you, I would never be unfaithful to him at all, Ted. If he only loved me, I'd be completely faithful and try my best to make him happy," she said, blushing to her roots again.

Ted kissed her on the mouth long and heatedly. It surprised Mandy a bit, but his kiss, his suddenly embracing arms felt so, so good to her. Her blood ran in warm currents through her veins now, and she felt wonderfully hot and delicious tingles going through her. She briefly wondered if it was wrong. This man was her stepfather after all. But then, was he? Her mother, his wife, was definitely missing and may very well be dead. So if that were the case, they really weren't related at all.

Her blood began causing sweet, delicious tingles all through her for the very first time. Was she like her loose mother after all?

Ted stopped kissing her then and said, "People are really complex, complicated, Mandy. Your mother has had serious issues. In the end, I realized she was a really sick woman who needed treatment, but she refused to get it. In the end, Mandy, her beauty was her downfall. I don't think it'll be yours."

"Thank you, Fat, ah, Ted, thank you so much."

Then he grabbed her to him and began kissing her more and more heatedly and then fumbled with her dress buttons and straps.

She said weakly, "Oh, don't, Ted, Teddy, this is wrong, so wrong," and then as he was still kissing her, she began kissing him back.

Then he said, "Let's make love, my darling, my beautiful, beautiful jewel, my darling!"

He grabbed her to him and pressed her body to his. He had rippling muscles, and Mandy felt herself floating and melting with desire at the same time. Then he grabbed her up and held her up in his strong arms and carried her up the marble stairs to the bedroom he and her mother had.

Mandy had never been inside it but briefly remembered the rutting, animal-like lascivious noises and sounds that had come from it when her mother had entertained her many lovers.

Would she bleat and cry out in some sort of frenzy like her mother did? She didn't care anymore! All she knew was that she was on fire and wanted Ted so, so much.

Suddenly with the lights still on in the large silken bed, Ted began taking all of her clothes off and all of his own too. To her untrained eyes, he looked so beautiful naked with his tanned, muscular body. His dark chest hair was thick and wavy. She felt deliciously smothered in it! His large, hard penis fascinated her, and she played with it and stroked it. Then, with his kissing, caressing her, it was inside her.

There was a bit of pain, and she gasped a bit and then nothing but deep, deep, voluptuous pleasure. Their bodies merged as one, and she felt as if she were drowning in sheer ecstasy. She was panting and moaning and then they both climaxed, and she thought she had died and gone to some sort of profane heaven of bliss.

Her small fingers and longer nails scratched his back, and suddenly, she felt she were all grown up now. She was a woman now, not some silly little girl whose mother had never loved her! She was a woman in her own right now!

She and Ted could live together as lovers forever and ever. When she was older and if her mother was indeed dead, they could move somewhere and marry and live, as far as she was concerned, happily ever after.

Then she looked at herself briefly down there and touched herself and looked at her fingers and they came up blood red. Oh well, that must have been what the bit of pain was about; she'd been a virgin until tonight. A silly childish little virgin and now she was not. Now she was a real grownup woman with all the desires of one.

She wondered if she'd really be as Ted had said, even more beautiful than her mother someday. If she were, good, then Ted would always be entranced by her.

She knew from her mother, a woman's beauty could be used to bind men to her. But her mother had been a fool, a complete fool with the powers of her own beauty wasting it on many, many men who really weren't entranced by her, just rutting animals as her mother had behaved like a rutting animal herself with them.

No, she'd have far more class than her mother about it. Then looking at Ted beginning to doze off and how beautiful a man he was. She felt his penis, and surprise, surprise, it began to harden again in her hand. Something inside her told her this was a marvelous opportunity for her to learn a very valuable lesson.

Ted was really more than half-asleep, but his penis was red and hard. Something immemorially old handed down a long, long line from mother to daughter from some distant immemorial source told her what to do next. Here was a man, a beautiful, godlike man to learn from, to kiss and taste and suck delicious pleasure from.

As if possessed, her face slid down his hard, hairy body, her tongue licking the wonderful skin and hair and then kissing his organ and licking it, and she began sucking it and loved the sweet, salty taste of it.

Her face ensconced between his hairy thighs, his penis, slowly savoring it and he moaned in pleasure. She began fingering herself, giving herself pleasure for minutes that seemed molten eternities of mad, red pleasure and passion. Then with a hoarse bellow, Ted came, and she lapped up the sweet, sweet juice like nectar to her.

So this was what a man was like? Oh, she loved it. Swallowing the juice down, so now his seed would be a part of her always. She really could do that all night if she want to. She wondered where, besides her whore mother, this had all come from, this level of desire. This seemingly inborn knowledge of how best to please a man!

Ted kissed her burrowed blonde head and fell rapidly asleep and began snoring a little. She looked at him, and Ted looked so satisfied and happy in his sleep. She knew inside, her mother in her marriage to him had never made him so happy and satisfied.

If her mother were still alive somewhere and came back, she'd fight her for this handsome, godlike man. And she knew she'd win that battle. Her mother, dead or alive, was a fool and she was not!

Then, with Ted beginning to drift deeper into slumber, she began to see a gauzy white light in a far corner of the bedroom. Oh, oh, she well knew what that was about.

Mandy was one of those very rare human beings who could see ghosts or the spirits of the departed materialize in front of her. Ever since she was very little, she had never told her mother about it. What was the point with her? But she had told Delia and Delia had been very afraid for her.

"Ya got the sight, girl! Ya got the sight all tight! Ya got a conjure eye just like I heard your granny had and her mother afore her. I knew when you were born here in ya Ma's bed with a caul on your forehead and eyes you'd have the sight all right! Ya got to ask God to protect you always 'cause not all ghosts are good!"

Eight-year-old Mandy had laughed at Delia, wide-eyed in fright, and said the ghosts she saw so far were all friendly. They kept her company a lot in the big, empty house. She trusted the dead, so far anyway, than she trusted the living.

But even before that early age, she knew from somewhere inside her that not all ghosts were good. One early evening, she had been in bed and a form had materialized in front of her of a black-haired, black-bearded man dressed in old pirate's clothes. He had a patch on one eye, and in her head, she could hear him roaring and screaming at her.

And when the translucent form lifted a big silver cutlass over her, she screamed in fright. Then another ghost materialized between the bad pirate and her in the bed. It was an old woman with long silver-white hair. Incredibly, she wasn't that wrinkled and her face, though gaunt, was still somewhat pretty. She held a shining crystal in her right hand and held it over the now furious pirate. Then with silverfish rays coming from the crystal, the pirate ghost quickly disappeared completely.

She only smiled lovingly at little Amanda and placed the shining crystal in her little hand. She said to her, "Keep this crystal, my baby. If you see the pirate or any bad spirit again, just shine the crystal over them and the light will dissolve them."

Puzzled and frightened, Amanda said to the ghost, "Who are you? What is your name? Are you magic, like a witch?"

The lady smiled at her and said softly, "Who am I, little Amanda, I'll tell you later when you are more grown up. For now, I must go. But you can see spirits or ghosts. It's a gift. I could too when I was little. You come from my blood a long, long time ago. Remember, when you see ghosts, there is nothing, nothing to be afraid of. I'm always watching, protecting you. I'll tell you much, much more later."

Then the kind lady ghost also melted in some white light and disappeared. Since then, Amanda could see the spirits but was never afraid of them. The light that Amanda was seeing in the far corner of her mother's bedroom materialized into the old, still pretty lady she'd seen before in her early childhood. The ghost waved to her. Amanda got up from the bed, slipped her dress on loosely, and went to her.

She heard the soft voice in her head say, "We must speak now, Amanda. Come out with me into the hall. This man must never hear you talking to me. Now come. I'll tell you everything."

Only then did Amanda take in the long black shimmering dress the ghost wore with the arms and the dress itself trailing along the floor wispily. She looked dressed as a witch or that lady she really liked from the television series, Morticia Addams from the Addams Family.

Unafraid, Amanda followed her out into the hallway outside of the bedroom. She kept her voice low so Ted wouldn't hear anything. She knew that was important. The ghost stopped at the end of the hallway and smiled at Amanda again. She had a beautiful smile still, and Amanda suddenly thought that this ghost, when in life, in her youth, was probably a very beautiful woman.

Reading her thoughts as Amanda approached her, the ghost said, "Aye, yes, Amanda, when I was young, I was very beautiful. I caught and held the eye of the king of England, I did, and that was no small feat with that one, I can tell you."

Amanda said, puzzled, "What do you mean? What country and king was this?"

"England, midear, jolly old England. And the king was the tall, manly Charles II of England. Through my affair with this king, you descend from both him and me and some other important lords and ladies of seventeenth century England. My name was Lily. I was half English, half gypsy. I had long black hair, green eyes, and red, red lips. I was doing my gypsy living near a tavern of England, and this king came in in disguise as a commoner."

"He looked at me as if transfixed. I knew he was the king, despite his disguise and gave him glance for glance. He was so handsome, he made my young blood start to course with fire in my veins. You felt that sensation this night with your stepfather, Ted. Wasn't it magical? Anyway, I'm here now and I'm having this talk with you because you have become a woman tonight with this Ted. A woman with all the yearnings and passions passed along to the women of my and the king's line. Also, you are in a great deal of danger now."

"I am in danger? Why, how? Surely not Ted! I think I love him!"

The ghost almost jeered at her and said, "Oh, you love him, the man who took your virginity at fifteen, and there is the matter of your missing mother too. Isn't there?"

"What about her? What are you trying to tell me now?"

"Just this, Amanda, this Ted does not love you. You are a delightful toy for him, nothing more. Listen to me, he'll whore you out to his rich clients for a pretty penny. He doesn't love you! And he most certainly didn't love your mother. Fascinated with her, yes. But in the end, her wanton ways drove him mad and so she disappeared several months ago!"

"Is she alive or dead, where is she now?"

"Never fear, dearie, come, I'll show you. But first you must take a loaded gun from the den where Ted keeps his guns and rifles."

"But he keeps them locked up in the den."

"Never you mind that now. I'll help you. I was a powerful gypsy witch when I was alive and I still, in death, have my powers. And then we'll go to the cellar together. With what we shall discover there, your life will be in danger from Ted."

"You mean he killed mother?" Amanda said, a sick, ghastly feeling in the pit of her stomach.

But she followed the ghost downstairs into the den. The den was, like the rest of the mansion, darkly beautiful with oak and teak paneling and a luxurious blue Persian rug on the floor. Following the ghost, she went to the cabinet she knew contained Ted's guns. Amanda, as if to show Lily, shook the doors of the cabinets. They were, as she knew they would be, heavily locked.

She looked at the shimmering ghost and said, "See, I told you so."

Lily laughed at her and said, "Look!"

Lily put her right hand upon the heavy locks to the cabinet and the locks, all three of them opened automatically. Amanda looked amazed at Lily and said, "How did you do that, Lily?"

The ghost only said, "Power, my line's power from my lifetime as a witch long ago. Now, grab a gun, they're all loaded. Do you think you know how to fire a gun?"

Mandy said, "Of course I do! I've seen Ted practice since he came here!"

So she took a small gun of the three guns there. Though it was the smallest, it felt hot and heavy in her hand. She put it in a dress pocket and then said to Lily, "Now what, Lily?"

"To the cellar, girl! To the cellar!"

Amanda got the chills up and down her body. So that's where her mother was. But when her mother had first disappeared, the police, despite Ted being a high-priced corporate lawyer and seemingly knowing everyone in the law and legal community, had inspected their luxurious mansion from head to toe, including the dank and musty cellar.

When she'd been very little and Delia had been very busy cooking and doing her housemaid duties, Amanda had, out of keen curiosity, snuck down the two flights of cement stairs into the large, dank, and gloomy cellar. Its walls were also cement and rough stone.

The place had many cobwebs. One naked light bulb shone on eerily for all the large cellar. The corners were shrouded in darkness. Delia had told her repeatedly not to go there. There were rats and maybe bad spirits down there. She saw there were large trunks, some closed and some open on the jumbled floors.

As she went down, she looked at some of the clothing in the opened trunks. There were men's clothes of an earlier, possibly Edwardian time and what seemed like decayed silk dresses were in them too. The clothes did not look like any she'd seen anyone wear in her time and place. She guessed now, years later, that some of the clothes came from the Antebellum South.

And then she saw something that frightened her totally. Coming out of one of the misty, moldy, darkened corners, some dark mist moved and came together. It formed itself into a very angry-looking black man with bloody chains on his hands and feet. He wore rags and looked directly at her like he wanted to kill her!

She took off right away and screamed and screamed, and Delia came running down the cellar steps and scooped her up and hugged her to calm her fears. Crying hysterically, she told Delia just what she'd seen. Delia just shook her black head and said, "Girl, yous only little, but you got the sight all right, like your mother's mother had. You can see things other people can't. You see a haunt, the ghost of a slave who probably was killed or died here. I thinks he's mad at all white people now, even little girls like you. You must stay away from this here cellar. It's got haunts and rats and mice! Stay away from it now, ya hear! I find you ever go into that cellar again, I'll a-going to spank you or even switch you. You knows yo mother would let me do that if you is bad. Now you be good. I promise you, you stay out of that cellar and that nasty old ghost won't come and get you. Ya hear now. Come on, we's going to pray from the Good Book. That will keep the haunts far away! Now listen to me and obey and be good!"

After Delia had read her the Lord's Prayer out of the Bible, Mandy felt much calmer and never ever even thought of going into the cellar again. She did have a few nightmares about the black man in the cellar, but they soon subsided.

On windy nights sometimes in her room, she did, she imagined, hear some muffled shrieks and wailing coming from the cellar, but she soon came to ignore it, hoping it would stop. No one else in the house ever seemed to notice such disturbing noises from the cellar, and until now, the whole memory of the dark cellar had faded gradually away.

But now she was following a ghost into the frightful cellar. But she trusted Lily and she did want to find out what had happened exactly to her mother. She did not owe her mother much in life, but she felt she did owe her that much. After a childhood of neglect, there was no love for her beautiful, debauched mother. But there was a primal tug inside her to discover her mother's fate.

Whatever else she was, she still was her mother and she guessed she did owe her that much. But if Ted really had done away with her mother, that would be horrible and she would be in imminent danger from him. She was glad Lily had gotten her the gun. Could she ever use it on Ted, even if he threatened her life?

She had really fallen in love with the beautiful man and now this! How awful!

When her mother had disappeared, she had briefly wondered if Ted had had anything to do with it. Her mother's intractable, wanton behavior was truly horrible to him after all. But Ted, her handsome, wonderful stepfather couldn't have been involved, she thought. He couldn't! But now, guided by Lily, she was going to find out, for sure!

The darkness of the cellar was overwhelming except for Lily in front of her who seemed to emanate a silverfish luminescent glow of her own. She saw Lily point her hand above her and a single light bulb above on the ceiling blazed on.

Lily looked directly at her and said simply, "Follow me."

Following behind her, Amanda became aware of an awful, decaying smell, sort of like a rotting garbage smell. She didn't remember such a horrid odor being there when she'd last been in the cellar as a small child. She was sure she would have remembered it if it had been there.

Then she heard the sound of rattling chains and groaning and out of the dark, dank corners of the cellar, black shapes moved toward her and Lily. Lily clapped her hands three times out loud and said, "Vanish now! Do not disturb us here!"

The wavering black shapes suddenly dissolved into the general gray, nebulous darkness of the cellar and the moans and sounds of chains vanished too. Lily turned toward her and said, "Don't mind them. They won't disturb us now."

"Who are they, and why are they still here?" she asked Lily.

"Just some poor slaves your several times great-grandparents didn't want to free at the close of the Civil War. So they left them down her in chains and let them die of thirst and hunger!"

"Oh my god! How cruel, how cruel! No wonder they haunt the cellar and hate white people now!"

"Cruel indeed, my Dear! You have good ancestors and bad for kin. I'll explain things to you after I show you where your mother is. Now come with me."

They walked across the floor in a diagonal way, and Lily led her into a gray corner of the cellar. The corner was covered with some loose dirt. Ironically, there was a small shovel nearby.

Lily looked at her and said, "Dig here. It's time. It's time."

Mandy, as if in a trance from the ghost, took up the shovel and began to dig and dig determinedly. She didn't dig too far when some distinctive odor both of decay and some acidic substance permeated her nostrils. She struck a white powdery substance and knew it was lime powder. She kept on digging and then she uncovered some bones.

When she dug up the skull, she knew it was the battered-in skull of her mother because of the still long, golden hair attached to the top of it. When a skeletal hand was uncovered, she knew the glittering ring on the ring finger was her mother's wedding band with Ted. Yes, he had killed her and buried her with lime to help dissolve the evidence of his foul crime. She wondered why he hadn't just divorced her mother after all. God and half the county knew she had given him more than enough reason to divorce her.

But then her quick mind thought, *If they had divorced, what about the money and property between them?*

"Yes, honey," the ghost said as if in an aside to her, "Ted chose to kill her because he wanted no scandal and her wealth and property too. He also, too, had his eye on you, his beautiful, virginal stepdaughter."

"What should I do now, Lily?"

"Why, obviously, call in the police and get out of this house before Ted awakens and finds you! Now!"

But then, Mandy heard some hard footsteps coming down the cellar steps. Lily said, "Be smart, girl, now, be smart. Use the gun I gave you to save your own life! I'll talk to you later!"

Ted had awoken, hurriedly put a bathrobe on, but she could see he was naked underneath. Funny thing, he didn't look shocked or upset at his bloody secret being found out, uncovered, so to speak. He just looked at her smiling, still seductively handsome with his big, deep blue eyes at her.

"Hey, Amanda, don't tell on me! You, of all people, know what your mother was a whore who disgraced you and me with her degraded, depraved life. I could take it no more, and yes, I settled the score, and she can disgrace me and you no more!"

"So you killed my mother! Look, I'll bet you knew what she was and did before you two were even married! The whole city of Dupree, Virginia, knows what my mother is, was. Yes, she was a whore, but you shouldn't have killed her! You're a murderer!"

"Listen, I'm a good lawyer and there isn't a jury which will convict me with first or even second degree murder when I tell of her disgraceful life. Her whole legion of lovers from here to Toledo for God's sake will testify to that! I couldn't take it anymore I tell you!"

"Divorce was the only solution, Ted, murder is wrong! Don't you know that?"

"Does what we did upstairs in your mother's bedroom mean nothing to you? I love you, Amanda! I'll really dispose of the remains this time. I'll sell the house and we'll move far, far away somewhere, and the day you turn seventeen or even sixteen, I'll marry you! With your mother's disappearance and probable death, you're not my stepdaughter anymore. We can marry!"

"And live happily ever after? Like a fairy tale? I thought that, too, when we were making love upstairs! But now, no! No! You killed my mother! How can I tell you won't kill me, too, someday?"

"Here's how, Amanda! Can't you tell I love you now?"

With that, he threw off his bathrobe and, naked, embraced her and strongly enfolded her into his hard hairy body. She struggled for a moment, but with the delicious tingles of rapture his rippling muscles and hair and kisses were creating, she felt her resolve melting in her ecstasy, her newly awakened erotic ecstasy at his body, the male scent he had.

This was wrong, so wrong, she felt. He had killed her mother! But, like a being possessed, her coming rapture and erotic joy overpowered her and she melted into his kisses, his body. They fell to the concrete floor and began making frenzied love only a foot or so from her mother's newly disinterred remains.

Amanda, possessed by total erotic frenzy, grabbed and stroked his erection and massaged it almost playfully. Then she burrowed her face into his chest and muscled form and began sucking his hard, long, beautiful penis as if it were the sweetest stick of candy.

The heat, the taste of it, drove her into a near delirium of pleasure. And then he came in her mouth and she swallowed it as if it were honeyed nectar and then climaxed herself. Now she definitely had a part of Ted inside her. Despite what he had done to her mother, she would never tell on him now. She'd move with him wherever he chose, and they'd marry later the day she turned seventeen. But then, Ted changed position; he shifted and was now on top of her and his two strong hands were around her neck, her throat, and he was beginning to strangle her. She gasped and gulped for breath.

He said hoarsely to her, "Sorry, baby, I can't let you live to reveal me to the police. I'll have to kill Delia too. I think Delia knows about what I did to your mother too. I've seen her looking at me with her big, accusing black eyes. Sorry, baby, this is just the way it goes."

In a paroxysm of life and death, her right hand grabbed the little loaded gun in her dress pocket and aimed it as best she could in her near-throttled state. She fired, praying the bullet would find its mark. Ted's lower head exploded in blood and bone and some brain matter and he collapsed on her.

Grasping for precious air, she tossed his trembling body off of her. Ted's eyes had a glazed look to them and lying on the ground so near to her, he barely garbled in gasping breaths, "You're your mother's daughter all right."

Then he gasped more blood up and collapsed totally on the floor in blood and flesh and bone and was dead. She'd killed him. But he'd tried to kill her. But she had loved him, no, loved him still. She still tenderly kissed his bloody neck and shoulder goodbye.

Then, with light and shadow shimmering in the air above her, she saw the ghost, Lily, reform above her. Lily reappeared and smiled at her and began clapping with her hands. Her fingernails looked very long and sharp, almost claw-like. Her withered pretty face beamed down at Amanda.

She said in a hard voice to the prostrate girl lying before her, "Well done, Amanda, well done, my girl. I knew you had the guts to kill him after all when he tried to kill you. What you did before with him, the lovemaking, the swallowing his seed, that was all part of your blood, your heritage from me and Charles II and a woman, Lady Villiers, who was even more hot-blooded than Charles and me. I must explain to you, you are different. You can see ghosts and move objects, too, with the force of your will and mind! You can psychically read people and their intents and can even predict the future. You can also will people to die or recover and live. It's all energy, child, and you, being of this extraordinary line have powers you never thought possible."

Mandy lay still stunned and said, "If my mother was of this line, too, what did she do with her so-called powers in her short life?"

"Girl, your pathetic mother wasted her powers in a sordid life of sheer debauchery. Well, with such hot-blooded forebears, some of my descendants have too much eroticism, too much sexual energy, and they can become the slaves, the pawn of it, rather than using it and their other powers in a more constructive way."

"Your mother was such a one. Ever since she was very young, fifteen maybe, it was one well-muscled man after another. She got pregnant with you and, you guessed it a long time ago, didn't even know who your father was. Your father was a distant cousin to your mother, and neither of them knew of the cousinhood as my descendants are spread quite all over this region of the South and some other areas of the country, too."

"But he carried the powers of the line, though, he was too uneducated and unaware to use them. But your mother carried intense powers and so did he. Hence, you were born with more powers than either parent, as sometimes happens entirely at random. He was young, good-looking, and well built. That's all that really mattered to your mother at the time."

Beginning to sit up, Amanda said, "You told me you had a daughter by this king. What happened to her?"

"Well, the king was so taken by the beauty of this baby girl, he openly acknowledged her and had nurses and tutors raise and educate her and make her into a proper lady. My daughter's undoing was the hot blood she got from me and Charles. At sixteen, she had a mad indiscretion with this villier's son, who was also by the king. This woman was a ruthless courtier and actually allowed them to marry early. It was a way, to her, of getting my daughter's considerable dowry and doubling up the royal blood in her line in the next generation."

"Oh, wow, incest now! No wonder I'm so screwed up!"

"Please, you are not screwed up, girl. Just realizing your powers!"

"Anyway, just read your history. Close breeding and even occasional incest was never a stranger to royalty. It kept their lines pure and their wealth in the right families they wanted. Anyway, the lines grew and prospered with the blessings of this king and later his brother James. Unfortunately, because these Stuarts were Catholic or too Catholic for the Peers of England, they were kicked off the thrones by Protestant Hanovers and so the reign of the Hanovers began. Finally, a bunch of nobles and peasants, too, with my lines behind them moved to Virginia and became very rich planters and what became Jamestown's upper class later."

"This is incredible. But what happened to the women if they couldn't control themselves like my mother?"

"Well, the more extreme ones were disgraced, sometimes burned as witches or put in the stocks or gaols as loose women and whores. Sometimes, as in Ted's case, they were secretly murdered by their enraged husbands. Most of my female descendants knew enough to at least try to control their libido for their husbands' sole gratification. I must say, some very happy marriages resulted from it. Though sometimes the men died from being too worn out from their wives' nightly demands. Sometimes, too, doctors' skills being what it was back then, a number of the women died in childbirth, too. But for the heightened health, hardiness, and the libidos, there were always plenty of descendants, too."

Finally standing on her feet, Amanda asked, still crying, "What am I to do now."

"Call the police now and show them everything. Being a minor, though with rich assets, I can tell you your mother had two nearest relatives. One, Lavinia Mannon, is your mother's aunt. She is a rich spinster and a very Catholic Catholic. Yes, dear, some of my Stuart descendants are either Catholic or its nearest religion Episcopalian. She'll raise you strictly in a good Christian home. If you choose her as your legal guardian, you might learn to control your tremendous libido as well as learn some of the finer things of life."

"The other great-aunt of yours, Eliza Mannon, though old, has more than her share of your mother's failings. The two sisters cannot stand each other. If you choose her, you'll never learn either discretion or self-control or even, possibly, self-respect. And then there is the question of your mother's estate and inheritance to you as her only surviving child. As you may or may not know, it is to be awarded to you on the attainment of your eighteenth birthday."

Amanda only looked at her dazed and said, "This is all just too much for me to handle now, Lily."

"Please, you must pay careful attention to what I am now telling you. Your Great-Aunt Eliza consorts with dead people. Some of my descendants can see and communicate with the dead as you can, but your Aunt Eliza carries it to unhealthy extremes."

Looking at Lily's wavering, ghostly face, Amanda laughed at her and said, "Oh, I get it, she has affairs with the dead! I never even knew that was possible."

"Trust me, dear girl, it is. It's all a question of energy, its uses and dangers, too."

"Wow! This Aunt Eliza sounds positively trippy!"

"Take my advice and choose Lavinia. She'll be good for your character! Trust me in this, all right! Now, call the police! Just say you killed Ted in self-defense after he tried to throttle you. fortunately, your neck and throat area have the fresh and highly visible bruises of his murder attempt on you. Do not worry in the telling of this. They'll believe you and the murder of your mother will be labeled on Ted as it should be. I really must go now! But don't worry, I'll be watching over you always!"

With that, the ghost vanished, and Amanda climbed slowly up the cellar steps and called the police from the phone in the den.

As she nervously told the dispatcher everything (except the part about Lily), she started breaking down and sobbing tremendously. When the police arrived, she tearfully told the police everything, pointed them in the direction of the cellar, telling them what they would find there. Then she broke down in mad, hysterical cries.

She was shortly taken to the station and then was seen and given a sedative by a female attendant there. They gave her a rough bed at the station, and she fell blissfully sound asleep with only some nightmares of finding her mother's grisly remains and then seeing Ted's handsome face shatter from the bullets. She cried in her sleep in her sleep and then woke up feeling more calm and centered.

A police doctor examined her physically. With the examination, they asked if Ted had ever touched her sexually. She said calmly, totally matter-of-factly, "He made love to me a few times. He didn't abuse me, I was willing, though he did come on strong and seduce me at first. I only killed him when he tried to throttle me. I mean it was self-defense and all."

The police and doctor were a bit shocked by this blasé confession of an affair between such a young girl and her stepfather, but then, really, not that shocked. In their line of work, they had truly seen it all. They did feel very sorry for her, though, for being such a victim to a monster. They ordered her a most nourishing breakfast. After that, they questioned her again as to what exactly had happened and, satisfied with her answers, turned her over to Children's Protective Custody.

For despite what she'd told them and what she had experienced, she was still a child, an innocent child on whom young womanhood had suddenly been placed like a malignant growth on her, her innocence suddenly as shattered as her seductive stepfather's now dead face.

Clearly, something must be done to help the poor girl-child-woman fast!

Three Months Later

While the police and detectives thoroughly investigated her, her home, her school life, and gathered the remains of Ted and her murdered mother, she was placed in a home for troubled adolescents.

She was medically examined with great skill. From what she'd told the authorities about her relationship with Ted, the examining doctor was relieved she showed no early sign of pregnancy. At just fifteen, that situation would have been very messy for her and her life on top of everything else going on. She had a few sessions with a judge (no jury) to whom she told her story of what had led to her fate.

She was found completely innocent and not involved in her mother's murder and that she had shot Ted in total self-defense. Ted was ruled the murderer and Amanda's near-murderer too. Ted's business clients were shocked at the denouement of his seemingly bestial character, but life goes on. Case very much closed.

Her mother's own lawyer, a Mr. Anthony Gray, took her case and appraised her of her situation. There was a sizeable inheritance involved when she attained her majority. But until then, a guardian must be appointed for her. He told her of some distant cousins who seemed uninterested in taking her. Then he mentioned two great-aunts.

One, a Lavinia Mannon had expressed an interest in having her live with her and becoming her legal guardian. The woman's younger sister, Eliza Mannon, had expressed no interest in becoming her guardian.

"One thing I must tell you, if you do come to live with this great-aunt Lavinia. Coming from your rather dysfunctional home and your late mother raising you as she did with no care or concern for your moral character and growth will be a very different experience for you."

"So I've been told," Amanda said to him, though not telling him Lily the ghost had told her so. She really didn't want him to think she was crazy.

"Look, my dear young lady, everyone in the city knew about your unfortunate mother's loose ways, even bringing her most casual lovers home to parade in front of her innocent child. And from your own admission, you said at the tender age of fifteen to having affairs with your murderous stepfather, Ted, before he tried to kill you as he had your mother."

"No, you don't understand, sir, it wasn't casual to me. I think I was falling in love with Ted. I knew it was wrong, but he was so handsome and manly, I don't think I could really help myself."

"Well, if your great-aunt Lavinia does take you in, you'll learn a whole new behavior. This woman, though old, is a virtual paragon of Catholic rectitude. She'll teach you what your late mother failed abysmally to teach you, virtue and self-control and self-respect, too."

"Hey, you have me wrong! I do respect myself plenty!"

"A self-respecting fifteen-year-old girl does not have affairs with her own stepfather! But I consider all that your mother's fault. Enough on that, though, you must promise me that if this Aunt Lavinia does take you in, you will obey her and be on your best behavior!"

"I'll try, I'll try. But I've just been through a terrible ordeal in which I lost my mother and stepfather and you tell me about this unknown great-aunt Lavinia, who sounds very strict to me. I suggest that, considering my trauma, I just try living with her and taking just one day at a time. I think it'll be a big adjustment for both her and me."

The lawyer, Anthony Gray, smiled at her and said, "I agree with you. Both of you will have to adjust to each other. But, remember, this is the nearest you'll come to both what's left of your family and the chance to learn correct, normal behavior so you don't become what your mother was. All right?"

"Hey, sir, my mother did not raise me well, I know, but she was still my mother, and please don't put her down for behavior I think she was born with. I think, at some instinctual level, though she never showed it, my mother did love me. I mean, she loved me enough to have me, rather than just getting rid of me when she discovered herself pregnant. I mean, she could have done that, whether it was legal or not, very easily and no one would have been the wiser either. But she went and had me, so whatever you say about what an abysmal mother she was to me, I at least owe her my very life. So please don't put her down to me anymore because even though she left the care, love, and nurturing of me to Delia, our maid, all-around cook, at some level, too, I did and still do love my mother! I don't want to hear another word about her loose morals or anything! It was behavior I don't think she could really help. Some people are alcoholics. Some turn to drugs. My mother's downfall was sex, but she may not have had any choice, really, in the matter. I guess it's how some people are born. Oh, by the way, how is Delia? I haven't heard from or about her since this terrible case started. I want to get back in touch with her soon. She was my real mother surrogate. The only one I could turn to for healthy, mothering love and support."

"Delia was completely ruled out as a suspect in your mother's murder, and she was completely shocked and revolted by what happened to Aurelia and to you. She told me to tell you she sends her utmost concern and love to you."

"Good, someday when I'm on my own, Delia can come live with me. You know, she was more of a mother to me than my real mother was."

"Good. But until you are on your own and grow up, please allow this Aunt Lavinia a chance to care for you, to hopefully love you and teach you the right way to live."

Amanda started crying suddenly at the thought of all she had lost, her mother, Delia, even that no-good murdering Ted. After she had regained a little more composure, she said to the lawyer, "As I said, it'll be a big adjustment for me. But I'll try, just one day at a time."

Amanda left the office to take the taxi hired by the Home for Troubled Adolescents to take her to her lawyer back to the home. While there, she'd made no friends. The other teenagers of both genders had heard word of just what had brought her to the home. While most of them were very troubled young people, they really didn't want to befriend a girl who'd shot and killed her own stepfather, even if it was, purportedly, in self-defense.

One young girl there, Heather, who'd been taken sexual advantage of by her own abusive father was somewhat sympathetic to Amanda initially. However, when she'd drawn Amanda out a bit and had asked Amanda about possible sexual abuse by her older stepfather, Amanda's totally blasé attitude to her sexual encounters with Ted, even telling Heather that while the man had murdered her mother and, in the end, had tried to kill her, too, she'd said as if discussing the weather to Heather, "Ya, I know he shouldn't have touched me that way, but I must confess my stepfather Ted was as handsome as the devil and seemed to know how to give a girl a real good time!"

Heather, who'd been her father's sexual victim since she'd been eight or nine, had been shocked and had ended the conversation very quickly. It wasn't that Amanda had killed her stepfather, but her blasé, nondescript attitude to the whole sex part was very disturbing in a girl so young.

Bur noticing Heather's reaction to her, Amanda had explained a bit of her dead mother's totally debauched life, and how, because of that, she considered sex in one's life no big deal at all. One should go about one's life as one wanted to. Just avoid disease and unwanted pregnancy, that's all.

While Heather's own mother had been far from pure herself, she found Amanda's late mother's lifestyle shocking in the extreme.

Her own mother would never have dared to cheat on her father. He'd have killed her if she cheated on him. What troubled Heather so much was that her mother had obviously ignored all signs of her father's sexual abuse of her for years.

But Heather had told the other kids in the group home all about Amanda's colorful background and no one tried to be friends with her there after that. Amanda didn't seem to care too much, though. She though most of the kids there were weaklings or wimps for having put up with the abuse they'd been victims of for years. Whereas she had done something about it and had saved her own life thereby. Sometimes, late at night, some of the younger kids there still cried for their mothers, and Amanda just shrugged and thought how weak they were. To her, life was for the strong and the strong only.

She herself didn't miss her mother at all. Aurelia had never been any sort of mother to her anyway, so why cry or grieve for something that never was right to begin with?

She kept to herself anyway there and read voraciously books that were in the home's library to pass the time.

She'd been told that when her guardianship would begin then so would her schooling begin, too. Concerning that, what if it didn't work out between this strict Aunt Lavinia and her? What then?

She just hoped that it did work out because being a ward of the state really sucked big time. She really came to hope she could have a nurturing relationship with Aunt Lavinia and to develop new ways in herself. But she had a sinking feeling that it was too late for her to change and become the good little girl they all now wanted her to be.

What were a dying Ted's garbled words to her, "You're your mother's daughter!" were words of both a curse and a prophecy, and it was already too late for her and she would become like her mother.

But she vowed one thing, she would give herself a chance to change and grow up, somehow, normal. She would give herself that chance, anyway.

Three Weeks Later

At first, she had found her old great-aunt pleasant and welcoming. One could easily tell she'd been a very pretty woman when young. She'd formally welcomed her into her large, old, luxurious house. Where her late mother had had one very capable servant, her Aunt Lavinia had several: A professional chef named Marcel who did cook delicious meals. Two maids, Rita and Marjy, and a steward who did odd jobs about the mansion, Fred.

When she'd been introduced to her great-aunt at her house by her lawyer, Anthony Gray, the aunt had been warm and welcoming and had even embraced her and had kissed her on the cheek. Then, the lawyer had left, leaving the two of them together and the aunt had pointed to the large luxurious parlor with her cane.

When they had entered the parlor, the aunt had sat down at one end of a shining mahogany table and indicated with her cane for her to sit at the other end.

"Dear, dear Amanda, we must have a talk so we can understand how you are to live here and the rules of the house for your conduct here."

"All right," Amanda said with that sinking feeling in her stomach, her guard suddenly up.

"First off, Amanda, this. You probably have heard from Mr. Gray, the lawyer, I am a deeply religious person. I love Jesus Christ and the holy sacraments of the Holy Roman Catholic Church. I expect your conduct to be as a virtuous young lady in the fullest sense of the word. I'll buy a complete wardrobe for you. There will be fine clothes and dresses in whites and pastels if you wish. But nothing at all immodest. And please, no makeup at all until you turn eighteen."

"If you are to live here, you will be a modest, virtuous young lady. You will have the best private tutors money can buy. I find public and even private schooling can be a breeding place of sin and illicit passion for young people who seem so hormone-driven today."

"Because of my extreme arthritic knees and joints, I don't go to church, but every Sunday, a priest comes here and hears my Confession and then gives me the Holy Sacrament of Communion. I expect you to learn from a priest and open your heart to Christ and Mary, the Holy Mother."

"Hey, wait! Hold on there, Aunt Lavinia. I've never had religious counsel or training in my life. I don't even know if I believe in God, OK? I don't want this religion, your religion, being forced down my throat by you or anyone! I may be only fifteen but I think I've grown whole years older in my home with my late, murdered mother!"

"Ah, that's another thing, Amanda, while you are living here, you are not to mention or talk about that loose whore, my niece, your mother!"

"What? What!" said Amanda, shocked beyond belief!

"You heard me! You know what your late mother was! A painted, perfumed Jezebel whore! And it'll be my mission to save your immortal soul from her wanton ways! If it's not too late already! I have the reports, I read them, sick to my stomach about what happened between you and your own stepfather! Your stepfather took unnatural advantage of whatever innocence you had and then tried to murder you to hide his murder of his wife, your mother. If you hadn't wisely hidden a little gun and used it when you did, he would have murdered you too! I just want to save you from all the sordidness you witnessed with your mother and were raised in."

"If you'll just give me a chance, Amanda, I can turn you into a fine, very respectable, and virtuous young lady of culture and refinement. You'll live here under my tutelage until you turn eighteen. Then you can go away to college if you qualify and that is your wish."

"But I won't be going to school before that, just private tutors?"

"That's my plan for you, my dear. Absolutely no corrupting schools and young people in your life. Oh, you'll be kept quite busy with the studies your tutors will give you. For pastimes, I have a wonderful library here and radios which are tuned into wonderful classical music. I listen to them myself."

"But no other young people? I mean, with my poor mother's reputation, I really didn't have any friends at school. But I would like a chance to see other young people for possible friends. Friendships are part of a normal life, a vital part of growing up."

"You mean you want to meet other young people, young men, too, I take it for dates, maybe?"

"Well, yes, isn't that part of growing up, too?"

Her aunt nearly laughed in her face as she said, "You've grown up already in all the wrong ways! From what I understand, your stepfather really didn't have to try that much to seduce you! By your own admission, you succumbed to him quite willingly, too willingly! Do you want to become a woman like your late mother?"

Amanda nearly cried at that and said, "No, no, no! I want to be a good, normal, healthy, young woman. And I don't want to hear another word about my mother from you! I think, at some very basic level, my mother did love and care for me. She had me and kept me, at any rate, when she could have very easily gotten rid of me when she discovered I was on the way. And a lot of her bad behavior I don't think she could help. Some people have the wrong brain chemistry or hormonal imbalance and, as a result, are highly sexed and cannot control their behavior. I think, no, I'm sure, my mother was one of those people. So please don't defame her to me again. I loved her."

Her aunt sneered at her as she said, "People can always control immoral impulses and behavior. One always has free will to sin or not. Free will, dearie, free will! Anyway, not another word about your late mother, that, I will admit, most unfortunate woman who certainly paid the price for her sins and indiscretion. The ultimate price, really, and I never want to see you someday paying yourself and for the same reasons. Just stay with me and I promise I'll try to honestly love you as my great-niece and everything I do here will be for your own good, believe me, dearie, for your own good. Besides that, I think I'm one of your few remaining relatives who seems to care about you and your welfare and wanting to see you become a better person than your background has permitted so far."

Her great-aunt took her cane and hobbled over to her and hugged her and said, "Give me a chance, dearie, I promise you won't regret it," and then kissed her affectionately on the cheek.

With butterflies in her stomach and remembering the counsel the ghost Lily had said to her as well as the fatherly concern and advice of Anthony Gray, her lawyer, she hesitantly said, "Yes, Aunt Lavinia," and kissed her wrinkled old cheek back.

On her first day there, her great-aunt had shown her about her marble and mahogany and teak mansion. Even before Amanda had formally moved in, Lavinia had Rita, one of her maids, with Amanda to town and she had been measured for her new wardrobe.

The dresses chosen were beautiful, even luxurious whites and pastels but were also with high buttoned-up collars, no décolletage at all, and were long enough to cover her ankles. When Amanda had objected to Rita that she wished for something a little more modern, Rita had pulled her aside and said, "I been with Miss Lavinia for twenty years, and when she gives me orders, I obey. And she told me real specific what kind of dresses she wanted for you."

"Beautiful dresses, you will admit, but nothing immodest at all. Remember, just give in to her. It'll be much easier for you to live with us. The Missus is a holy lady she is and despises sinful behavior and all."

Amanda's eyes opened wide and said, "Well, I guess so!" and closed her mouth and really wondered if this move was right for her.

Aunt Lavinia had shown her all the rooms in the house, which was very luxurious indeed. She also showed her a room called the Ancestral Room. In it were the old portraits of many of the old lady's ancestors and Amanda realized suddenly that at least some of the old portraits were some of her ancestors too.

"Here are the portraits of some good, God-fearing people!"

"But what about some of the ones who weren't so good? I've been told some of my ancestors weren't so good!"

Aunt Lavinia smiled coldly at her and said, "I don't know who told you that, but I admit, some of our ancestors were wicked, ungodly people indeed. But you won't find their portraits on my walls. In fact, if I knew they were bad, I crossed their names out of the family Bible."

"Including the ones who let their slaves die of hunger and thirst in the cellar of my house rather than free them?"

Her aunt whirled on her and grabbed her by the collar of her dress, "Who told you about that bad deed?"

"Oh, I learned it! That cellar is haunted now by their ghosts!"

"Oh, you're one of those who sees the dead, are you? Yes, some of our family can do that. And in the old times, some of them were burned for it as witches too! But, Amanda, I won't have that here in my house! The church says not to have anything to do with the dead except to pray for them. To have concourse with spirits is a mortal sin and can take you down to hell. Do you understand that, girl?"

"No, I don't!" Amanda said, beginning to be angry. "I don't think it's a sin or a curse. Imagine what we can learn from the spirit world!"

Lavinia Mannon grimaced as if having a stroke and said, shaking, "None of that nonsense in this house, Amanda, whether you have this 'gift' as you call it or not."

"My younger sister, Eliza, lives and breathes spirits and behaves, I believe, most indecently with them too. Maybe you should go there to live. How would you like that?"

"All right, Aunt Lavinia, I'll stay with you, I guess. Mr. Anthony Gray told me Aunt Eliza expressed no interest at all in having me live with her and really could do nothing for me morally."

"Good, glad that you see my point. My sister Eliza is a most selfish person. She loves the dead, not the living. Trust in me, Amanda. I intend to give you a good, wholesome, loving home."

And then the old lady embraced her and Amanda said, embarrassed, "For which I am grateful, Aunt Lavinia. Most grateful."

Then they went over the rest of the house, and Lavinia introduced her to the rest of her servants and staff. All the servants were gray-haired and middle-aged, if not older. Before introductions, her aunt told had told her that she'd had most of them, like the maid, Rita, many, many years. The servants were soft-spoken and several smiled at her at introduction.

The next day, the ritual of her new life began. At 7 A.M., Rita or another maid would come into her luxurious bedroom, gently shake her awake if she were still asleep. The two maids would help her clean, shower, and then dress for the day. From a girl who'd had no direction or care from her late mother to a routine like this was a startling change.

But Amanda didn't protest. She was here to learn proper morals and ladylike deportment after all. After morning ablutions, the maids led her to the dining room in the parlor. She was seated at one end of the marvelous, thick, shining, mahogany table and her Aunt Lavinia was seated at the other end.

Another maid, Shirley, served the most delicious hot dishes of breakfast. Usually, there was some sort of warm oatmeal or a bran cereal ("For the fiber, dearie, it'll do your insides good and keep you regular, too," Aunt Lavinia had insisted). Then either French toast or really scrumptious omelets with spinach, mushrooms, and cheese.

Coming from a professional chef, it was all most delicious. Her aunt had told her to please eat. She was a growing young lady and too slender as far as the aunt was concerned.

Before each meal, though, her aunt said grace and Amanda folded her hands and prayed with her aunt for good manners' sake.

But saying grace at the table was about as far as Mandy went as far as organized religion went. When Aunt Lavinia preached Catholic religion at her, which she did frequently, Amanda would just nod to appease her and let the admonitions go in one ear and out the other.

On Sundays, her great-aunt would have her attend the Mass with her in her parlor near the den with the priest she'd hired to give her the sacraments. Father Julius Minot was a gray-haired older man. When he preached the sermon, Mandy found it boring, usually. To her great irritation, after the Mass, dressed in his usual priestly garb, she would be left with this priest in the den. There would be a book of Catholic catechism between them and he would lecture her on Catholic theology.

This greatly irritated her. She had told her aunt at the beginning that she didn't want religion forced down her throat. But not to cause friction in her new home, she seemingly went along with it. In her third week of such catechism, the priest christened her in front of Lavinia from a bottle of holy water from his church with the admonition that she must now lead as sinless a life as possible in honor of Jesus and Mary.

Aunt Lavinia, afterward, gave her a gift of several thousand dollars and let her keep $100 of it and put the rest in her bank account in her late mother's bank in Richmond. She also gave her a Catholic Bible, some crystal rosary beads and the priest would instruct her how to pray the rosary. She also gave her a new book of Catholic saints which also had specific prayers to them in it.

After the baptism, the time of her home-schooling began and Aunt Lavinia sent for two tutors to give her various academic lessons. They were a various Mr. Rutland Unbridge and a Miss Rowena Cathbent. Both of the tutors were in their fifties and had gray-white hair and some wrinkles. But they were both competent teachers in their respective fields of English, Math, Biology, and French and European history.

Every weekday now had them coming to the mansion and tutoring her for several hours each day in their respective fields of study. She was also given copious amounts of homework with the schoolbooks and notebooks that were given to her. In the main, she was glad of the work and the tutoring. It really made otherwise tedious days go by. Plus, they both brought her news of the outside world.

Aunt Lavinia did not believe in television ("Too much sin in the television shows today, dear") and kept the several radios on in the house to classical music stations. One thing her aunt did have, a wonderful library near the parlor. The library was composed of classical books of fine literature. Her aunt did have some excellent texts.

All of the books were not on the index list of banned books of the Catholic church. With the books from the library and her new lessons of homework to do, her mind was kept very busy indeed.

The gardens about her aunt's house were beautiful, full of roses and daffodils and various other flowers. When Amanda had asked her aunt for permission to help Fred, the older gardener in his work, her aunt had said she could come out and enjoy the gardens any time she chose. But no, she could not assist the gardener.

For a young lady of her station now never got her delicate hands dirty. If she wanted some healthy exercise, her aunt had sent some servants into town and they had returned with a stationary bike and some very light two-pound weights and some jump-ropes and put them in her large room.

After Mandy finished her homework and some reading of one of the many of the library's excellent books, she did some half-hour or forty-five minutes of exercise. Then around 9 P.M., Rita the maid would knock on her door, come in, and draw a hot, fragrant bath for her and Mandy would bathe and in it while Rita had poured some fine, fragrant oils of rose and lavender bath oils in.

After the bath, she toweled dry, got into her white silk nightgown, said some newly learned prayers, and went to bed. In the soft, luxurious four-poster bed, Amanda had no trouble falling asleep. Sometimes, her sleep was disturbed with some bad dreams and nightmares about finding her mother's remains in the cellar in her original home. She also sometimes saw Ted's handsome face shredded by the bullets she'd fired at him in total self-defense. Even though he had tried to kill her to eliminate a witness to the crime of her mother's murder, she still had mixed feelings about Ted.

He had been previously a loving stepfather to her. And when he had broken those boundaries and had so fiercely and heatedly made love to her, she had admittedly responded in kind, glorying in his godlike masculine beauty. She didn't regret having made love to him; it was wonderful. But she had learned something from it. Not to trust too much if one fell for a man's purely physical charms.

For ultimately, Ted had never been in love with her, indeed, had tried to kill her to cover up his murder of her mother. The ghost Lily, in instructing her to bring a gun to the cellar, had saved her life indeed. When she woke up feeling bad from those disturbing dreams, she realized that was her life then, definitely not her life now, and upon reflection, she found herself growing more and more fond of her Aunt Lavinia who really was doing so much for her now.

Every day now, she learned and more in her lessons. Her Great-Aunt Lavinia grew more and more effusively affectionate to her. To Amanda's astonishment, the old lady really did seem to begin to love her. It seemed, despite her vast wealth and placement in Richmond society, she'd been a very lonely old lady, and now in Amanda, she had a family and a safe person to love, nurture, and cherish.

Four or five months after Amanda had been there, Aunt Lavinia had been chauffeured uptown in Richmond, only saying she had some legal business uptown. When she left, with Amanda waving to her from the front porch, Amanda vaguely wondered if the legal business uptown concerned her at all. It was true, the old lady had given her a safe, orderly oasis after the horrible tragedy of her home had ended in bold, bad seduction and murder.

She had structure in her life now. Yes, Aunt Lavinia was very strict with her and her upbringing. In fact, lately, another tutor had been brought on board to refine her manners and to teach her elocution as a young Southern belle. Why, just yesterday, with Lavinia beaming over the academic progress reports from her tutors, the old lady had said that she was very proud of her and her progress. In fact, she'd said that if she continued her progress there that when she turned eighteen, she would give her a grand debutante ball to which, to her shock, other young ladies and young gentlemen from the best families of Richmond would be invited along with the parents, of course.

"It'll be your formal introduction to fine society, dearie, and my showing Virginia society how I've grown to love you and accept you as what you are to me now, family. A debutante ball will be fine right before you go to some good college or other to pursue a career. Oh, despite my strictness I've raised you in, Amanda, a debutante ball also signals to other grand families that their sons may now court you as a member of my family. And we are a great family in this area."

Amanda said, beaming with pride herself, "I've heard it said, Aunt Lavinia, we go back to royalty in old England."

"Well, some of my family said that when I was a young girl myself. Though I only had a family tree set up for our Virginia roots. As to royalty, I guess it's possible. Anything is. Now, you be a good girl while I take care of some legal business uptown."

As she left, her aunt kissed her on her cheek and her head, saying how proud she now was of her. Later that day, while Amanda was all alone in her room studying some of her lessons from her tutors, lying on her bed, she saw a ghost. It rapidly assembled from light beams before her eyes. It was Lily!

"Hello, my child! I have not shown myself to you for a long time, watching you and watching over you!"

"Why haven't you manifested to me for a long time now?"

"Because you've been very busy adjusting to your new home here and to your Aunt Lavinia. I'm very proud of your progress, and Aunt Lavinia is now pretty proud of you and loves you!"

"I know and I'm glad of that. Aunt Lavinia can be formidable It's just, with no other young people here, it's kind of lonely."

"I understand what you mean, child. I have a solution for that, though."

"What do you have in mind, Lily?"

"That tonight in a dream, so to speak, I open your mind to another ghost. Oh, don't be alarmed, this ghost is young and handsome and quite charming. He's an old associate of your Aunt Eliza. He died a brave Confederate officer at that horrible battle of Gettysburg. I recently spoke to him, and he seemed very interested in meeting you."

"From what you've told me of this great-aunt Eliza, she is on most intimate terms with her male ghosts, and you suggest the same salve for loneliness with me!"

"Well, darling, if you don't have the living around, resort to the dead! And you can clairvoyantly see and communicate with the dead, as did many in your ancestral line, as I previously explained to you!"

Amanda smiled at Lily and said, "So you expect me to have a ghostly wet dream, so to speak, out of this!"

"I know how lonely and frustrated you are here. When I came upon you at your home and your raging hormones were being stoked by your murderous stepfather, Ted, in a total and dangerous misalliance. Believe me, you are much safer dealing with a ghost lover than a living one. Just make sure to be subdued and reasonably discreet. Your Aunt Lavinia would not like this sort of arrangement at all."

"How well I know that, Lily, she thinks communicating with the dead is all devilry! She is so Catholic, it's ridiculous. Still, she's a very good woman, and I don't want to upset her in this matter. And you said this former Confederate officer is handsome and died young? And died young at Gettysburg? I studied that in the course of the Civil War. Many thousands of soldiers on both sides died there. It was horrible!"

"And many of them were so traumatized by the awful way they died that many thousands of them are still here earth-bound spirits, unable or unwilling to move one."

"So in this dream or this experience, this ghost will feel just as good, just as physically enjoyable as a vibrant, living man?"

"His first name is William, dear, and yes, he'll feel delightfully physical for you. Don't worry, he'll visit you tonight."

"In more ways than one, I suppose. Yes, Lily, I am interested in meeting him. In my position here, beggars cannot be choosers, I suppose."

And then Lily kissed her a ghostly, immaterial kiss on her cheek and faded totally from view.

That night, Rita, the maid, looked questioningly at her as if she knew something was up. Maybe it was because Amanda had insisted that a lavender and rose oil be put in the hot, steamy bath water that night. For that night, Amanda wanted to be totally clean and to smell really fragrant to meet this supposed young male ghost of her dreams.

Well, really, living with Aunt Lavinia as she did there was no possibility of mascara, perfume, or makeup of any sort. She was really curious about this whole new mad adventure. She did not doubt Lily's word for a moment. If she had said someone, someone very handsome and interesting would come tonight in her dreams, then Amanda knew intuitively she would.

Why, oh, why couldn't her Aunt Lavinia be normal and send her to a good school to meet and make friends with boys and girls, too? Instead of isolating her and keeping her like some rare and hothouse flower who would so easily perish at the slightest contact with the outside world. She knew her Aunt Lavinia had come to love her, and for that she was glad and grateful.

But when a month ago, Amanda had raised the issue of contacting her former maid and really loving surrogate mother, Delia, to come over to the mansion and visit her and how much she still loved Delia, it all went wrong.

Aunt Lavinia had said tersely, "No contact at all from your former life at that sordid house, even if you loved her as some sort of substitute mother. You have come so far from that terrible place and foundation. Sorry but I just cannot chance it for you and I really wish you wouldn't contact, write, or call this woman, Delia, ever again. In fact, it is very much against my express wishes if you do."

No matter how much she pleaded with Aunt Lavinia, that was that. So in a way, because of the abnormal was she was being raised here, Aunt Lavinia was sort of forcing her into this bizarre situation.

A date, if one could call it that, arranged by one ghost to another ghost!

Yes, she supposed it was bizarre, but consider the clearly bizarre way her great-aunt was raising her here now. She wanted male company. She hoped this new ghost was handsome and would feel strong and warm in his possible kisses and embraces.

That night, she went rapidly asleep and found herself being erotically held and embraced with her so handsome stepfather, Ted. He was naked and so was she in his former bed. Though at their last encounter, he'd tried to strangle her, still, it felt so good to be with him again. His naked body and strong hands and arms thrilled her warm, tingling body with his own. It was every bit as extraordinary and erotic as it was before.

And then, as the climax was building like some slow, hot fire in her loins until she thought she'd scream, he rolled her over in the bed, and she suddenly realized the man she was with was no longer Ted. Yes, this man looked younger. He had the same black, black hair and blue, blue eyes which her stepfather Ted had had, but this was a very different young man.

This one was an even handsomer young man with a smaller nose and clearly defined chin and profile. Somehow, she knew what his first name was. Then the orgasm hit her like an exploding volcano and she screamed, "You are William, William, William!"

"From your Aunt Eliza's world."

At that very moment, she felt herself being grabbed and roughly shaken! William and the bed they shared vanished, and with the tremendous screaming and vicious pulling, she opened her eyes to a living nightmare.

Her Aunt Lavinia was shaking her viciously, her face twisted in seemingly murderous rage and fury! She was dressed untidily in her best turquoise nightgown and bathrobe. The maids Rita and Margaret were there looking startled and upset at the scene they were witnessing Aunt Lavinia, seeing Amanda was finally fully awake, slapped her with surprising force for an old, supposedly weak, old lady! Her face was taut and white with fury!

"I know what you were doing! Slut, whore, You were committing a mortal sin like a common whore of the streets! Mortal sin, mortal sin, mortal sin! In my house! Just like that born slut of your mother who is undoubtedly burning for her many sins in the unholy fires of hell this very moment! I tried, oh, I tried so to save you! But when I came upstairs to see you in your sweet, unsullied sleep after what I'd done for you, what a horrid scene should greet my eyes but you in sleep, caterwauling and moaning like a cat in heat in a backyard alley! Well, you had no physical lover, that I can see, but what were you seeing in your sleep, what were you doing?"

Suddenly, Amanda was transformed from shock and horror at her Aunt Lavinia to red-hot rage and fury herself.

"I was doing what you forced me to do because of your crazy and fanatical beliefs! I had a handsome lover in my dreams and he was making love to me like no tomorrow! You isolated me from the world and any sort of a normal life and girlhood, you! If I had friends my own age in a normal school like most kids and not isolated with you in your demented holier-than-thou purity, it wouldn't have happened! I have feelings, wants, needs like any normal girl! Maybe what my stepfather told me as he lay dying before me was true, I am my mother's daughter all right!, And you want to know something, my mother had her grave faults, but she was a hell of a lot more normal than you'll ever be! And I don't want to be here one more moment longer! Take me back to the place I came from. I'll appeal to the courts to be placed with a new guardian! This time, a normal human being, not you!"

Her Aunt Lavinia gazed at her in wide-eyed shock and horror. She nodded to the walls of the room and then Rita and Margaret, the dumbfounded maids standing there like mute, silent figures and then screamed, "What have I done! What have I done but everything for this ungrateful girl! Everything to stop the evil seed from her whore mother from blossoming to fruition in her! But it's obvious to me, Satan has taken over her mind! But maybe it's not too late to save her immortal soul. Yes," a white, glazed look coming into her eyes, "I'll save her soul from Satan! You two girls hold her fast now! Hold her firm no matter what she screams or says!"

Almost unwillingly, knowing their jobs depended on it, the two buxom maids grasped Amanda's arms in steely grips. Her Aunt Lavinia tore the back of her nightgown offm and there was her back fully exposed! Her now clearly demented Aunt Lavinia ran from the room, and Amanda pleaded with the two maids to release her. That what her aunt and they were doing to her was wrong and illegal and she wanted out and she wanted it now, this instant.

The maid Margaret nodded in silent assent to what she said but still didn't release her, Rita said to her, struggling with her, "Well, you shouldn't have riled her up with your moaning and groaning like you were with a lover man!"

"You've been here long enough to know anything like that would make Miss Lavinia crazy! So just shut up and take whatever punishment, and there will be one, like the brave young woman you claim to be! Hell, you had enough guts to kill your stepfather yourself when he tried to kill you. You should have guts enough for this!"

Then, turning her head around, Amanda heard and saw her Aunt Lavinia run into the bedroom brandishing a long black whip! She couldn't believe her eyes, a whip, the lethal-looking whip looked like a big, vicious horse-whip!

"This was my daddy's whip when I was young and free and loved a boy he didn't approve of for me. He whipped me hard and it hurt like hell, but it saved my soul like I want God to come and save yours now!"

And then her aunt began whipping Amanda's naked back again and again until it hurt like no other burning, stinging pain she had ever experienced before. She cried, begged, cursed, and pleaded, but her back skin was being lacerated with the cruel whip and she knew her back was now bleeding and her back might have scars from this nightmare forever!

Then, as the pain went on, Amanda saw a figure materialize from the bedroom wall she was facing. He wore a Confederate uniform and was really handsome in a rough, dark-haired sort of way. It was the ghost she'd seen and made love with in the dream! It was William. Apparently, her Aunt Lavinia and Rita and Margaret didn't see him at all, He said to her in words only Amanda could hear, "Watch this, Amanda! No one treats a girl I like like this!"

And then he hit Margaret and Rita with a powerful fist in their faces and they both cried out and let go of Amanda. Then he punched her Aunt Lavinia who was too caught up in whipping her still. He also tripped her so that she fell hard on the floor. Amanda only prayed that this witch of an old lady had broken every bone in her body.

Both the frightened maids clutched their bleeding faces and then ran to their fallen mistress as she moaned and groaned and cried on the floor. Amanda quickly recovered her scattered senses and bent down and grabbed the whip from Aunt Lavinia's now weakened grip!

She said loudly, hoarsely, "I should whip all three of you bitches to death with this and see how you like it!"

But her Aunt Lavinia sprang up with the maids' assistance suddenly and cried, "Sinful, wicked girl!"

The two maids ran out of the bedroom and her Aunt Lavinia ran out too and took a key from out of her pocked and locked the bedroom door from the outside!

"I'll leave you in here with your wickedness and the ghosts who helped you just now! No food or water for you until you disown Satan and say you'll be good!"

Amanda, her poor, naked, bleeding back a very fire of terrible, shredded pain collapsed on the bed and fell unconscious in shock.

The last thing she remembered seeing was the face of the ghost William looking down at her most pityingly. Then blackness engulfed her totally. And her body, going into physical and emotional shock shut off all the pain and agony and the darkness which engulfed her was total and mercifully numbing all over.

Utter unconsciousness engulfed her in the cool smothering darkness but then, somewhere, somehow in this unfathomable darkness a hazy, silvery light engulfed her. She found herself on a tall pile of indescribably soft, deep silken furs and cushions. Somehow, her ancestress, spirit-guide Lily was there floating high in the air where she lay. Lily kissed her face tenderly, then she said, "So sorry this happened to you, darling. I honestly had no idea your aunt Lavinia was so unstable. But I did warn you to be discreet, didn't I? Oh, well, I have something for your poor, whipped-to-shreds back. With this ointment, your back will heal well without any scars. I myself made it and used it secretly on the backs of some prisoners who'd been whipped for petty crimes, like stealing a loaf of bread when they and their families were starving. Oh, there was a lot of that type of misery in Merry Old England. There was really no relief for the poor back then and many of those beggars turned to crime just to survive. I felt sorry for such criminals, for they weren't criminals to me, just very poor people who were totally destitute and starving. Anyway, this special ointment usually worked quite well on their backs. I often pleaded with King Charles to establish a public charity so the poor wouldn't starve, but the Villiers woman negated that real quick. She usually wanted a new bauble of new allowance for her or her bastards by the king. Anyway, I digress, my darling."

"Hey, but I'm in this dream, I think. How can this ointment heal now in the real world?"

"Oh, it will, dear, it will. My magic affects both dream and reality and it's all one and the same energy."

"Oh, you mean like how William hit the maids and Aunt Lavinia in my defense?"

"I'm glad he did that for you. From a slight acquaintance, he's developed quite a shine to you. He wants to help you and protect you like the gallant young Southern gentleman he is. He was a very brave and gallant Confederate officer."

Suddenly, Lily's cool, ghostly hands were rubbing a cool, cool ointment unto her very sore back. As she rubbed and rubbed the magical ointment unto her bruised and shredded back, all pain suddenly vanished and she felt so good and healed.

She suddenly said to Lily, "As I remember, my crazy aunt locked me into my bedroom suite from the outside. How the hell do I get out now?"

"That's so easy," said Lily's cool, mellifluous voice. "Just use your will, dear, and the door will break down. You'll be using your own inherited witch-power. Just press hard against the door and say and think, 'Release, release, release,' and the door will unhinge out unto the floor. It'll be the first practice session for you."

"And then what? How do I get out of my aunt's clutches?"

"You will discover, dearie, your now pitiful great-aunt will be in no position to stop you. You might, in fact, wish to say goodbye. She has a great secret to impart to you, and believe it or not, despite her violence to you and her religious craziness, she has done you a great service. And, remember, being able to forgive a wrong done one makes the wronged one a greater person."

"Thank you so much, Lily. And since he's nowhere here, thank William for trying to protect me too."

And then the cool, healing darkness pervaded her mind and senses and she was unconscious again in that darkness, dreaming unremembered dreams within a dream.

When she awoke some hours later, she was alone in her bed in her room. Her back was still a bit sore, but it no longer pained her. When she got up, she turned her head and looked quickly in her bathroom mirror. All her backside wounds had healed without visible scarring! Really, Lily's potion had clearly done its magic.

She brushed her teeth, showered, and dressed into an informal pink and white dress. Now, all she had to do was somehow get out of this locked bedroom and out of this sanctuary turned madhouse!

She'd call the police first and then her lawyer Anthony Gray, appraise him of what had just happened, and appeal through him to the courts to appoint a different legal guardian until she turned eighteen, and she came into her inheritance.

She really wondered if she could get out of this room turned prison by her own will and power or not? Well, Lily's potion had worked, and if she herself was indeed descended from her, maybe she did have some occult powers after all.

She went to the locked door and pressed and pressed screaming, "Release, release, release me now!"

She felt a great energy wave come bolting out of her body to the door. With a loud clang, the lock shattered and the door flew open. Now the thing to do was to get out and tell the authorities what had transpired!

Despite what Lily had said, she had no wish to see Aunt Lavinia, just get out. Putting a soft white cashmere jacket on, just in case the fall weather had cooled, Amanda got out of the room and turning the hallway corner, nearly rammed into the maid, Rita.

Rita had been carrying a full breakfast tray of toast, coffee, and an omelet with hash potatoes, and it smelled quite delicious. With everything going on in her dream and that morning, she'd been without food for a while and was suddenly famished.

Before the tray collapsed on the floor, Amanda grabbed it in her two hands. A very startled and disconcerted Rita said to her, "How did you get out of that locked room, Amanda? Oh, I'd rather not know. After your ghostly tricks last night, I think you very powerful indeed. Anyway, the breakfast is for you. The Mistress Lavinia had a bad medical turn last night. She cried hysterically over what had happened for hours and then collapsed blue and breathless on her bed. We called her doctor. He came over, examined her, and said she'd had a very mild shock to her system. He was most concerned by the bruises on her face, she told him she'd fallen on her face upstairs. He wanted to call an ambulance to take her to the local hospital, but she insisted she'd get better in her own bed and that was that. You know how stubborn and pig-headed she can be."

"I also know how brutal, even sadistically cruel she can be. I'm going to tell the authorities all about how you and Margaret held me against my will and she whipped my back with that awful horse-whip! You and Margaret and Aunt Lavinia, if she recovers, will see me in court!"

"Oh," said the maid, looking very worried, "she's real sorry about that now. By the way, how is your back? You seem to be mending quite well."

"My back, thank God, is almost miraculously healed. One of my good ghost friends applied a very healing ointment to it and it really worked! But even so, Aunt Lavinia shouldn't have done what she did to me and you and Margaret shouldn't have helped her. Don't you know all three of you can do serious jail time for what you did to me? It was not only sadistically violent but illegal too!"

Rita only nodded her head and said, "When you've been with Miss Lavinia as long as I and Margaret have, we know that here, Olympia Mansion, her word is law. And you set the mistress off with your wicked turning and twisting and moaning like you had a lover in bed! You knew it would upset her!"

"It didn't justify what she and you and Margaret did to me!"

"Anyway, the Mistress told me to give you breakfast and to release you. She wants to see and talk to you, explain herself to you. Please come with me and see her in her bedroom. She cried and cried and won't touch her breakfast. If you just walk out of here, as is your right after what happened late last night, she'll die. She'll refuse to eat and die. She's that upset! Please, Amanda," said the maid touching Amanda's hand and beginning to cry herself in a very plaintive voice, "if she ever meant anything to you as your own last family of refuge, please see her and talk to her! If you won't, as God is my witness, she'll up and die and that'll be on your conscience the rest of your life. Come on, she opened her home and heart to you and tried to make a decent young woman out of you. Come and forgive her if you can."

Grabbing some of the breakfast and hurriedly eating it, Amanda didn't say yes or no until she finished eating the delicious food. Then, nodding, she followed the maid downstairs to where Aunt Lavinia's bedroom was. She really didn't know if she could forgive her or not, but she could hear her out. Something told her her great-aunt had quite a tale to tell her.

Rita, the maid, opened the door for her to Aunt Lavinia's bedroom, and in the norning light and lamplight, Amanda saw Lavinia on her luxurious bed. She had some livid bruises on her face from her ghost William's fists when he'd stopped Lavinia whipping of her.

Her face was pallid, more wrinkled than usual and teary-eyed and tear-stained. Looking up at Amanda standing by her bed, she said in a quick, breathless voice, "I'm so, so sorry to have hurt you so last night, but when I caught you either pleasuring yourself as you were or cavorting with a ghostly lover as my sister Eliza does, I think I went a bit crazy. Either of those activities are a mortal sin. And if you should die in the state of a mortal sin, your soul is damned for all eternity."

"Die, you said, die?" Amanda said in a quiet, deadly penetrating tone. "Die? If my ghost William hadn't interfered and stopped you and your maids from whipping me, I very well might have died at your hands! It was the most severe pain and trauma I've ever experienced! But Lily, a now familiar ghost who was a gypsy-witch in her lifetime, rubbed my back with a magic herbal ointment and my poor back is mostly healed now with no scarring, thank God!

I'm going to tell the police and authorities what you and the maids did to me last night! I can imagine criminal charges will follow, and despite all your money and your good Catholic reputation, you very well might go to jail! I'm going to ask my lawyer and the courts for another legal guardian until I turn eighteen. I'm leaving here as of now and never want to see you again, you old religious freak of a witch!"

Aunt Lavinia burst afresh into wailing tears, almost whimpering as if in great anguish. Amanda only looked at her stony-faced, not pitying her at all.

She suddenly fired off, "All right!, Since my back is all healed now and totally without scarring thanks to Lily, my great ghost friend, I think I won't complain to the authorities about what you did to me, the vicious whipping and injuries. Though I really could have you and Rita and Margaret thrown into jail for it, I'm willing to let it go. But I'm leaving here and now and don't try to stop me. Let me have a new legal guardian, someone who isn't a religious nut like you are. So I can live a normal life for a girl my age with school and friends my age! Yes, that is what I want and will get it yet!"

Her great-aunt ceased whimpering and crying and said to Rita and Margaret hovering near her bed, "Rita, Margy, please leave me and Amanda now. I'll ring for you later. I have something very important to tell little Amanda here. Before she leaves me, if she will, I must have a very private talk with her now."

Worried-looking, Rita and Margaret left the room and silently shut the door on their way out. Now Amanda was alone with Aunt Lavinia. She was suddenly a little afraid of this suddenly pitiful-looking old lady. There was not a doubt in her mind that her Aunt Lavinia was stark raving mad.

Was it really safe to be alone with her in the same room? Suppose she, with the adrenaline-pumping strength of a madwoman, tried to overpower her and strangle her or stab he with a secretly hidden knife or even a large hairpin? When dealing with the mad ones, anything was possible, after all.

"My dear, dear child, please don't up and leave me like this, I beg you! For you see, however I wronged you by whipping you, I was doing it to help save your soul from Satan. Also, you and I really are family. We're much closer in blood than you realize!"

Amanda looked at her suddenly, startled.

"What do you mean by that? You're only my great-aunt after all. That isn't really close at all. Almost like second or third cousins, it that, even."

"No, no, no! Sweet Jesus in heaven, must I tell you my eternal shame? I suppose I must divulge the whole sordid story. When I was fifteen, a young man, a very handsome young man, oh, he was some sort of cousin from the Radia side of the family, secretly kissed me all over and then forcibly had his way with me! He shortly left for parts unknown, and I was left, you guessed it, pregnant with his seed. I tried so hard to hide it and took all sorts of things to stop it, but it never worked. Finally, my parents caught me throwing up in the morning and guessed the horrible truth! I was ashamed and horrified! Both my parents were very religious and strict."

"Hey, wait a minute! It wasn't your fault! This male cousin of yours forced himself on you, poor Aunt Lavinia, he raped you! Didn't they understand it wasn't your fault!"

Aunt Lavinia stared at Amanda's face blankly and said, weeping, "Understand, you ask? They only felt total repulsion and complete shame for my sinful condition! My poor mother wept and wept and wept. Daddy took his horse-whip and whipped me and whipped me all over until, I say, he drew blood. I think he was trying to kill me and the unborn baby by the blows. Finally, Mother forcibly intervened after I had passed out. When I woke up, I was in bed being tended by Lucille, my Mammy who tended my whip cuts and bruises and tried to hush me as I cried and cried and cried about my awful situation."

"From that day on, I was locked shut in my room with only good Lucille to tend to my needs. My parents told my school I'd been diagnosed with TB or something contagious and dreadful and they had sent me away to some TB asylum in Arizona for a cure.

In those days, one either died from it in one of those asylums in deserts in Arizona or one was miraculously cured by the very dry air and intense sunlight."

"My parents never really spoke to me ever after until the baby was born. Thank God, Lucille knew something about childbirth as I was ridiculously young to have a baby and nearly died in the birth. My mother came and recited the rosary as I was screaming in white-hot agony with the pain and said that my pain was punishment for my sins. I almost died giving birth. I passed out anyway, and when I awoke, the baby was gone and I was told by my mother the baby was still-born and they secretly buried the body somewhere and I should just forget all about it."

"At any rate, while my parents never really expressed any love or tenderness for me after that, I was allowed to leave my prison-room and go back to school with some tutoring. But what my parents told me rang very false about the baby. Finally I cornered Lucille, and she broke down crying and swore me to the utmost secrecy. The baby was born alive and was a beautiful blonde little girl. She was given to Edwina, a much older married sister of mine as she and her husband were long since childless. They christened the baby girl Aurelia and guess what, yes, she was your mother!"

Amanda looked at her horrified. "Oh my god! My mother! That means you are my grandmother, not just great-aunt!"

"Yes, darling, I am your secret grandmother. Because of my shame in the whole thing, I never contacted my older sister her husband or little Aurelia. But on those rare family parties and reunions, I saw her and them and she was so, so beautiful. I never dared tell her I was her real mother. What was the point of reviving that old scandal? It would utterly defame me, my parents and little Aurelia. But unfortunately, when Aurelia became such a beautiful young teenager, as you must know by now, she was headstrong and really liked the boys way, way too much! But there was never anything her supposed parents could do to discipline her and stop her downward, sordid spiral."

"By the time she was sixteen, her name was a byword for loose sex and sinfulness. Whenever I heard the gossip, I cringed and cried. It was like a knife piercing my very heart. I prayed and prayed for her and even had novenas said for her but, alas, to no avail. When she had you out of wedlock with never a word to anyone as to who the father was, if she even knew herself, I thought it was history repeating itself but what could I do? If I had interfered the sinful deception might be revealed!"

"My god," said Amanda, "it well might have been."

"Oh, I so, so wanted to come to her family mansion and shriek the truth to her and forcibly take you, an innocent baby though illegitimate like her mother, out of the atmosphere of depravity and sin that had by then become your mother's way of life. When she married that handsome lawyer, Ted, I felt things might really change for the good for both her and you. But alas, it was not to be. Your poor mother could no more stop her cavorting with men than an alcoholic can stop drinking without the help of God and the AA and medicine. She was damned and doomed!"

And then Aunt Lavinia grabbed Amanda's hand and so unexpectedly kissed it and said to her, crying volubly and breathlessly, "And the lawyer-husband turned bad himself, if her really wasn't bad to start with and murdered your mother to stop her sleazy, shameful ways, and later, he seduced you, his own stepdaughter, and when you discovered the murder and the real murderer, tried to kill you too. That you shot him before he could strangle you to death I say was the intervention of God Himself! Can't you see that? God wanted to give you the chance you never had for a good, decent life, child, you'd never have in your mother's clutches. When I heard about it, I immediately contacted the lawyer who was representing you to become your legal guardian. That, outside of my being your natural grandmother, which no one knows, I was a great-aunt anyway to you in what I must say is a family of very entangled branches, helped, too, as well as my reputation for clean living and loving the Lord. But in the South, remember, blood counts an awful lot. When you came here and we were getting along so well, I came to love you not just as a granddaughter but as the baby who was cruelly stolen from me."

Amanda looked at Lavinia directly and quizzically, "So when you caught me fooling around with an unseen spirit in the bed upstairs, with your beliefs and background, it must have driven you crazy!"

"Oh, it did, Amanda, it did! I had such high hopes for you becoming a good girl despite your mother's genes and influence! Now, I went crazy and whipped you with the same old lash my father used on me when he discovered I was pregnant! It's no excuse, Amanda, but I was equally shocked and infuriated as my Daddy was at me at the time."

With what her Aunt Lavinia had gone through in her life and the fact that she was her own and only grandmother and was totally sorry for what she had done to her, an overwhelming wave of compassion swept over Amanda, and she bent down to where Lavinia was lying in her bed and hugged and kissed her tenderly.

She then, inhaling the old woman's lilac perfume, said, "I forgive you, Grandmother, I forgive you."

Lavinia cried tears of joy and kissed her back. Then a serious look came over her face and she said, "There's something about the family you and I belong to, and it's something that, even at your young age, is already affecting you, unfortunately. I lied to you a little when I told you I didn't know anything about our family before its American roots. Well, I heard around certain family circles that we had important, even possibly royal ancestors in England. That's all grand and fancy and all, but in the blood, there's witchcraft. Some of the women of our family and a few men, too, can see and talk with the dead. Some can even do more with the dead, in fact. My own younger sister Eliza, in fact, prefers the dead to the living. She even has indecent relations with the dead and doesn't care who knows it. You may have already begun along that pathway!"

"Listen to me, Amanda! Leave the dead alone! The good souls are waiting for us up in heaven. The others you don't want to know, for they'll surely drag your immortal soul down to hell with them!

And while we're on the subject, I want to have a frank discussion about sex, yes, I said, sex in general to you! Oh, I realize in this so-called modern world, men and women have sex quite freely and often outside of marriage or even love and commitment. You saw enough of that with your mother's, ah, lifestyle."

"Well, honey child, my dear Amanda, what do you think a man, and most of them are all alike, will think of you if you give yourself so freely to him, not waiting to even knowing, never mind loving him or any word of marriage? Well, let me tell what he will think of you. He'll think you're just a cheap piece of action, and he'll forget about you for the next casual fling! And you'll be left with a big mortal sin to drag you down to hell in the next world and possibly the beginning of a baby, unwanted and illegitimate in this one! Well, tell me, Amanda, looking at your mother's short life, my poor, poor daughter, look at how she wound up! Her name was a dirty joke in this city and the whole of Virginia. Is that really what you want, honey?"

"No, Aunt Lavinia, it isn't what I want! But I think I'm too like my mother. I have her genes and all, but when I see a really good-looking, well-built man, I feel all hot and feverish for him and I sort of cannot control myself like the way I behaved with Ted, my murdering stepfather. I sort of can't control myself. I told you at the beginning I thought my mother can't help herself with men as she was just born that way. Well, I may be, too, with living handsome men and maybe dead ones or the spirits of ones, too. As to it's being a sin and hell and all, I just don't believe it, never did. Not if people are born that way, then God doesn't or shouldn't judge!"

"Oh, Amanda, Amanda!" Lavinia crooned at her. "Maybe some people in our family are born like your mother undoubtedly was. But there is such a thing as self-control, all right? And if you want to continue living with me in my mansion of a house with every luxury I can possibly give you, I want you, for you own good to have some respect for yourself and the whole inherent sacredness of your own body and try, in the name of the Lord, to please have some self-respect and self-control!"

"I'm also going to change some conditions here: if you choose to stay here, I'm going to send you to a private school in Richmond so you can have friends of your own age. My keeping you in isolation here was wrong. You need young friends and I will allow it. Just please do not embarrass me by your behavior, and I will tell you what I did for you while I was in Richmond."

"What?" Amanda asked, wide-eyed.

"I saw a lawyer, one of the best in the city, in fact and changed my will! Yes, honey, in my new will, I declare you my own and only legal granddaughter, and I'm leaving you most of my fortune and this mansion, Mount Olympias. With it and the money and mansion you will get from your mother's estate when you are eighteen, you will be very rich indeed. Now, if you want a good education and professional career in some field, I'll pay for that, too. I expect you will want that, too. You're a bright girl, and I respect you for that."

"Now, darling, we understand each other better, don't we? And no matter what happens from here on out, I promise, promise I'll never whip you or use physical punishment to control you again to control or curb you. What happened was highly unusual for me! I'm not a violent person at all, really. It's just when I caught you doing whatever you were doing with whomever you were doing it with, I snapped, snapped! It will not happen again! That I do promise you!"

"All right, Grandmother Lavinia, all right!"

"Oh, about that, just when it's between us, you may call me Grandmother and I love you for it. But when anyone else is present, just say Aunt Lavinia and that will do nicely."

"Will do, Aunt Lavinia, will do!"

Amanda kissed her grandmother again, feeling so good inside as now she knew everything; it felt good to love this old lady who was so blood kin to her. She could love and respect her as she never could her own dead mother.

She went upstairs to her room, her suite of rooms, she told herself, undressed, put her pajamas on, and fell into an exhausted and deep slumber.

Sometime in the night, she had a dream of the Confederate officer William, and he kissed her sweetly, lovingly, tenderly. Nothing else intimate transpired, but she did awaken smiling to herself. This William had treated her respectfully that night and he was so, so handsome.

Later that day, at the breakfast table she had a talk with her secret Granny Lavinia. She asked her if her former maid/cook/housekeeper as well as real surrogate mother Delia could be allowed to come here to visit her at this, her new home.

When Lavinia began to object, she said to her, "Delia isn't bad at all, Aunt Lavinia. In fact, when my stepfather Ted sent her away for the night so he could seduce me, she warned me about her suspicions about him and told, pleaded with me to be good, not bad. She always wanted me to be good, not like my mother. Whatever learning about God or good and evil, I learned came from Delia. She's a good, God-fearing righteous Baptist woman who gave me all the love and caring my late mother didn't I miss her terribly. What she found out later about what happened between me and Ted and how he killed my mother and then tried to kill me must have come as quite a shock to her. I worry that it's affected her heart or general health and state of mind. I have to bring her here, so I can show her I'm being raised right for once by a good, God-fearing woman who is my nearest blood relative, OK?"

"Oh, all right, all right, Amanda. She can come visit you. If she is as good as you say she is, I'll take the both of you out to lunch at some fancy restaurant in Richmond. You're a bit like me, I guess. When I was little, my favorite person and the one I loved the most was Lucille, my black Mammy. The woman saved my life in that difficult childbirth so long ago. Despite being a Southerner, I never had any feelings of superiority or animosity toward blacks. And in all your time here, I haven't heard you express a single cruel or disparaging remark about them. And as I with Lucille, in your house, this Delia was the one who really loved you and who raised you and loved you, too."

"Oh, during that time, when I was kept prisoner in my bedroom in those long, dreary months and months, Lucille was the one who not only took care of me but kept me sane, despite my parents' cruelty. She always told me things would get better for me once the baby was born. When I wouldn't eat, crying and being upset, she made me eat, saying I mustn't further punish myself and the coming baby, too. I'd told her about my male cousin forcing me, and she said that then this baby wasn't the result of my sin at all, the boy's sin entirely. Why, sometimes as I cried at night alone, she'd pat me, kiss me, and croon old black spirituals to me. She gave me more love than my own mother ever had."

"As I told you, I was my parents' mutual shame, but Lucille only loved me! Much later on, when I was middle-aged, Lucille died and I cried and cried and cried. I arranged with her family to have her buried near our family's plot at Jackson Cemetery with a big, fancy marble stone with her name etched on it. Sometimes, I brought flowers to her grave and cried and talked to her in the grave. No, I understand how you feel about Delia. Love has no issue with race or class boundaries. Love, darling, is love. You call your Delia today and invite her here at once. She can be a guest of honor, in fact!"

Later on, Amanda was delighted to at least and at last talk to Delia in her small home in the black section, Bourbonville, in Richmond. When her warm, earthy black voice over the receiver first spoke to her, Amanda started crying out in sheer joy.

After expressing how good it was to at least talk with her again after so long and how shocked she'd been over what had transpired that night in her house with Ted having murdered her mother and then trying to kill Amanda. Amanda cried and cried, the grisly memories appearing in her mind of her mother's earthly remains.

Then she blurted out to Delia, "You had your suspicions about Ted, didn't you, about his having killed mother?"

"I did, I certainly did! All your poor dead mother's old boyfriends didn't want to kill your mother! That woman was too much fun to them, and some of them could live high on the hog with her alive and all! No, I figured it was none of your mother's boyfriends who did her in. I figured it was Ted. But you know and I know, honey, if I went to the police with my suspicions, they would pay me no mind at all. Who I be to them, jus' an old, fat black woman who's just a maid and cook of the house? You know how it is, darling! And I definitely didn't want to leave you all alone with him that night! Didn't I warn you to be careful with that man?"

Amanda blurted out to her, "I wish I'd paid you more mind, Delia! I wasn't careful enough it seems!"

There was a shocked exclamation on the other end of the phone, and Delia said in quick and furious maternal rage, "Did that big, nasty man have his way with you? And you his own stepchild and just fifteen too?"

Amanda sobbed into the phone a muffled yes, and Delia asked, "Please tell me God Almighty you ain't pregnant with that cursed man's seed, are you?"

"No, thank God, Delia, no! And Aunt Lavinia knows what happened too and she understands how it was and he really took advantage of me. She's really wonderful, Delia! I'm beginning to love her. Anyway, get set for this, her chauffeur is driving me to you house tomorrow, I know your address, Delia, and he's taking you back to my Aunt Lavinia's house, mansion, I should say! She really wants to meet you after I told her how you were like my real mother and took care of me and loved me. I told her that whatever I learned of God and the good book and good and evil I learned from you! She's quite impressed. After she meets you here with me, she's going to take the both of us out to a fancy restaurant."

"She do that and I a black woman in a fancy white restaurant?"

"Delia, she can be real strict but in a good way. She told me when she was a child and young girl, she had a black maid she really loved. She told me because of that, this Lucille of hers, she herself has no real prejudices against blacks. And she is really important in this city. So rich and respected here, I don't think there'd be any burning crosses on her front lawn so to speak for her liberal beliefs. Don't worry, Delia, you'd be safe as her guest at a fancy restaurant.

Just wear your best Sunday church dress, OK? See you tomorrow, Delia. I love you, Delia and have missed you terribly!"

For the rest of the day, Amanda kept herself busy studying her courses she'd had with her tutors. Aunt Lavinia had said the school would get some feedback from her tutors as to where she was at academically and would get records from her former school when she lived with her late mother. They would use these records and records as to where to place her at the Regency School. It was the most exclusive high school in Richmond she'd be going to.

They'd also give her some tests, too, to better gauge her IQ for the school. That night, Aunt Lavinia came herself and kissed her good night. Upon her orders, Rita the maid no longer came and drew her bath for her. Amanda had drawn her own bath with the special soaps and oils Rita had used for her baths. Aunt Lavinia had said it was to give her more independence and to be treated more as an adult.

But Amanda knew inside it had been Rita had balked at further dealing with her because of the ghostly incident at the whipping. So the two maids were afraid of her, good, She'd wanted more privacy anyway. After Aunt Lavinia had kissed her good night and had instructed her to pray to be a good girl, she'd left for her maids and her own bedchamber. Amanda went to bed feeling relaxed, tired, and very fragrant and clean.

She was looking so forward to seeing Delia the next day. She was very certain Aunt Lavinia would like her enormously. In fact, she was hoping that Aunt Lavinia would hire the woman and add her to her staff to be Amanda's personal maid. Realizing how old and now arthritic Delia now was, if she became her personal maid, Amanda would keep her duties light.

No more cooking and cleaning. Just helping her dress in the morning and maybe make her hair in the morning right before school. Oh, yes, to make her a cup of her so soothing chamomile and valerian tea when her frayed nerves to her as they often did. That herbal tea mixture had always soothed her and usually sent her off to dreamland in no time when her mother's cavorting with her lovers had upset her more than usual.

Well, those days were now over. Her poor mother was even beginning to fade in her memory into a blank abstraction. Yes, she felt bad about what had happened to her mother. But it wasn't as if her late mother had shown her any concern or even faint love. It was too bad, really. Yes, her mother had given her life instead of secretly aborting her, and for that, Amanda was grateful but that was about it.

And her beautiful mother was fast becoming a not very important thought in her life now and that was all. That night, as she was beginning to drift off to sleep, she saw some luminous light in the darkness of her bedroom, and in a few seconds, the light solidified into the diaphanous form of Lily.

Lily smiled at her and went over near her bed and patted her on her head. She said in a silken, whispering voice, "Well, are you glad you came here after all? I'm glad you forgave your Aunt Lavinia for the whipping. It was terrible, I know, but you now know you triggered the nightmares from her past. She confessed that she's your real grandmother. Trust me in this, she will never whip you again or use any corporal punishment. No, not even a slap, even when you most deserve it."

"Look, Lily, I forgave her, OK? I suppose she's grateful for that."

Lily laughed like tinkling bells and said, "Grateful to you? I should say so. She really loves you, you know. She's wanted to know and love you since you were born, really. To her, you are the secret baby who was stolen from her."

"With her story, which I never imagined in a million years from someone like her, I felt so sorry for her. She's had a horrible past."

"Yes, indeed. Now she wants to make amends by giving you her most love. The maternal love she wanted to give her baby, despite the shame of her birth. Oh, by the way, in your dreams you might have a visitor. Someone you are just beginning to know."

"William?" Amanda asked.

"He just might drop by indeed. You made a powerful impression on that particular young man ghost."

"Well, he made a big impression on Aunt Lavinia and Rita and Margaret all right! He stopped their cruel whipping of me!"

"You know why he's taken such a fancy to you? Because you remind him of a girl he loved a long, long time ago. This girl promised she'd marry him and would wait for him. But then he was killed as were many thousands of troops at Gettysburg and trapped by their own death trauma and pain and thoughts of revenge."

"And then this great-aunt of mine, Aunt Eliza has sex with him and other civil war ghosts! Ugh! That's like necrophilia!"

Lily looked thoughtful for a moment and said, "Well, dearie, the dead can't get a girl in trouble like the living can. And let's face it, if a girl is halfway discreet about it, which your Aunt Eliza isn't, but she has enough money not to care what people think, a gal with sex on her mind can have a lot of fun. Look, your late mother got carried away with her sex drive and the living men. Now, I want you to get an education, which your good Aunt Lavinia will help you get and someday marry and have children of your own. Children who will carry on my line."

"But don't get obsessed with William or any other ghostly lover. Just be discreet and have some fun if you choose to. And trust me, a friendship with some secret, protective ghosts, as you have seen already can help you with living, earthly matters. Sometimes, it's even as simple and nurturing as having someone sweet and kind to talk to when you feel down. One can learn many things from the dead. Just don't get carried away and obsessed with them. Good night, darling."

And with that Lily vanished into the darkness, and Amanda curled into herself beneath her heavy blankets and drifted off to sleep. She had a very disturbing dream. She saw a scene that could have been one of Dante's lowest circle of hell. She saw men, mostly young, dressed in blue and gray uniforms shooting wildly at each other with pistols and rifles and stabbing and slicing each other swords and bayonets.

She saw guts sliced out of stomachs, blood everywhere, and even small groups of men blown to scattered pieces by cannon fire. She just knew it was the battlefield of one of the hot, sweltering days of Gettysburg. It still haunted the collective American psyche with its horrific and gruesome nightmares. Many thousands of Civil War troops being killed horribly in just a few days and the vast majority of the wounded to die soon later of their terrible wounds and, at that time and place, festering infections.

She saw mounds of amputated arms and legs at small primitive field hospitals. Then she saw a still handsome, bloodied Confederate officer she knew to be William, the William of her dreams, riding hell bent on a black charger. Somehow she knew at a deeply unconscious level that he was carrying an important message. A message for General Lee himself about how the battle was going disastrously for the Confederate side.

She felt it was important to William that he get this message to General Lee. Lee might think the battle irreparably lost and order his surviving troops out. Somehow she felt it was important to William to get this message to Lee to help save whatever lives could be saved for the Confederacy.

And then she saw a Union soldier taking as careful aim as he could muster in the chaos of the battlefield and shooting him with his rifle. She saw the top of William's head explode in blood, bone, and brains and he fell off his horse dead, the message forever undelivered and hence, the battle continuing on its relentless and very bloody course for both sides.

In her deep sleep, Amanda was crying for this William and also completely transfixed by the whole horror of this battle which would live in infamy in American history.

Maybe the whole Civil War was a terrible punishment from God on America for the unspeakable sin of slavery. Not too far from the house where she had lived with her late mother was a very old building in the town where she'd lived where she'd heard black slaves had been sold in Antebellum days. When she'd really read and thought about it, how whole black families were torn apart, especially mothers from their own children or even babies from their mothers' breasts on the sale block and how slaves were exhibited like cattle or horses for sale.

And then she'd read of the horrific punishments meted out to the slaves on the plantations: the terrible work and drudgery of the cotton fields, the whippings and even brandings with hot irons and mutilations for punishment.

Of how slaves considered too old and feeble to work or breed were routinely given a special sweet drink loaded with laudanum to put them to sleep permanently. Her gorge and mind at that time rose up in total nausea and horror. She could never pass that building without wincing in near-visceral pain.

No wonder, she thought, the ghosts of those chained, starved slaves had been so furious and revengeful in the cellar at her simply for being white. How could people have been so cruel and barbaric back then?

As she was remembering her past in the dream, she saw William again but in a time before that fatal battle. He was still in a Confederate uniform with a very pretty blonde girl in a period-piece blue dress down to her ankles. Her golden hair was blowing in the wind.

And then it came to her suddenly! This particular girl who was obviously William's sweetheart! Then in a second, as dreams go, she was this girl from long ago in her blue, long, fluttering dress in William's strong arms. He was kissing her passionately with his well-modelled red lips, and she was kissing him back passionately.

This William felt so real and he was so strong and so very, very handsome with his black, black hair and blue, blue eyes, looking a bit like her so devilishly handsome, late, murderous stepfather. They were lying naked together in the meadow under some close to the ground full bushes under some trees. The air was fresh and pure, the wind strong.

She rejoiced in William's strong, hairy chest and very muscular arms, kissing him on his face and neck and all over. His covering body caused ripples of erotic desire and physical ecstasy to burn her delightfully. As he entered her, she thought she'd scream in a paroxysm of climatic rapture!

He climaxed snorting like a magnificent stallion, and they were both melting in each other's arms. She suddenly awoke from this dream, and to her intense shock and joy, William was there in her bed naked like her and his ghostly body felt so strong and brawny and burning with passion.

She began kissing him again all over and he her. He said in a strong, smooth male voice with a distinct, even melodious Southern inflection, "You're mine, Katy, you are mine now and forever."

Alarmed, Amanda stopped caressing and kissing him and said, "Hey, William, I'm not this Katy from so long ago. I'm Amanda, and I'm from the state of Virginia of the twentieth century. I'm not that girl I saw in that dream with you. I am Amanda! And I think I could love you!"

Sunlight began coming into the bedroom windows, and William said to her, "You may be Amanda in this life, you're present life! But you were my Katy from a long time ago and you will always be my Katy. I will always love and protect you like I did before!"

Then with the room fully lit with the morning light, William vanished into the light and she was grasping empty air.

Well, really, it had been quite a night. Looking at her watch on her bureau, it was 7:30 A.M., and she was supposed to see Delia around 10:00 A.M. to bring her to meet Aunt Lavinia before all three were taken to a fancy restaurant in Richmond.

Washing up and showering and later dressing in a pretty pink and white spring outfit, she remembered bits and pieces of her dream and meeting with William. How even for a ghost, she was so very handsome and well-built. His amatory skills were outstanding. Just being near him gave her bubbling tingles of euphoria and ecstasy. Comparing him to her only other lover in her life, her late stepfather, Ted, was no contest at all.

While Ted had been a skilled Lothario, William seemed to be passion itself. There had been a simpatico to their lovemaking. And if what William said was true and she was his Katy reincarnated in this life in the twentieth century, then they were soul mates indeed.

She hurriedly ate a lavish breakfast near Aunt Lavinia. Aunt Lavinia worriedly told her not to stop the chauffeur-driven limo for anything in this Delia's section of town as she knew it was a slum section of Richmond said to be dangerous. Amanda smiled at her great-aunt and said, "Yes, Aunt Lavinia, I'm sure Vincent (the chauffeur) knows about finding safe streets and roads in Bourbonsville."

Bourbonsville was the slum and predominantly black and mixed-race section of Richmond. And her aunt's concerns were justified indeed. On hot summer nights in Richmond, there were not infrequent rapes and robberies, even murders in Bourbonsville.

One of Amanda's secret agenda was that in introducing Delia to Aunt Lavinia and hoping her Aunt Lavinia liked Delia enough to have her in her big mansion, she hoped Delia could be her personal live-in-maid in her aunt's luxurious mansion.

She really didn't want Delia facing awful dangerous and even possible murder where she was presently living and had been living for most of her life. Well, she said a silent prayer to Jesus and the Blessed Mother to spirit Delia to ease and safety in this beautiful mansion that put her late mother's mansion to shame. She felt, somehow, keenly, intuitively, that Aunt Lavinia and Delia would hit it off big-time.

Both women were up there in age. Both were good, religious women, though Delia was strictly Black Baptist through and through and Aunt Lavinia was fervently Catholic, she didn't think that would create any problems. Hell, most of the servant class in Richmond were fervent Black Baptists and most of their white employers were either Catholic or High Anglican.

And usually, both classes just accepted each other. That was how it was in the South. Whatever anyone believed in in the South, as long as they loved and accepted Christ, whatever one's Christian-based faith was acceptable and good. It was true that in some parts of the South, there were some people who were fanatically evangelical Protestant and disdainful of other people's faiths, that was a minority opinion, at least in Virginia.

Being the oldest state, there was a certain civility about different people's beliefs. Also, if a richer white Southerner had black servants and domestic help, there was a sort of almost benevolent attitude that as long as the servants were good and faithful employees, the white employer would help and protect them.

Of course, in the 1960s America, class and race were near well insurmountable attitudes that were unbreachable. Blacks often knew everything about their employers, and when Christmas and Easter came around, everyone in the house, both black and white, celebrated in good cheer with each other. As long as the order was maintained, there was a certain civility there.

The upper crust of the whites heard about the busing and the attempts at integration of the schools and universities and just shook their heads in befuddlement. Why, to them, would anyone, white or black, want to change anything that had, in their own minds anyway, worked so well to the benefit of both races?

In Richmond, only the lower-class whites used the N word, not the upper-class ones. But with the sometimes ferocious battles about integration and voting rights, at some level, though they tried to deny it to themselves, most upper-class white people knew that a profound change, a sea change as it was, was coming to the South and the pattern of their lives, both white and black would never, ever be the same.

Amanda really believed what Aunt Lavinia had told her. Because of her deep relationship with her Mammy, Lucille, she herself did not harbor prejudices against black people nor, for that matter, other non-white minorities.

"We are all indeed God's children, Amanda," she had told her not two days ago.

The chauffeur, Vincent, did know of the safer ways to go in Bourbonville, but Amanda could still see shabby houses and tenement buildings and many black children playing unattended by anyone in the cluttered streets. Finally, the limo pulled up to the address which she'd given him, and there was Delia in a slightly shabby blue-violet dress holding a pocketbook but still wearing her black flat shoes. Some things never change indeed.

Delia was smiling broadly at Amanda. She had one gold tooth in an otherwise flawless white smile. Amanda knew it was a genuinely gold tooth because her late mother Aurelia had paid for it all, in a very rare, to her, show of benevolence. Amanda hurriedly opened the door and ran up the rickety front wooden steps to Delia's fat, black arms and kissed and embraced her with all the intensity and fervor of a small child hugging and kissing her very favorite grandmother.

"Lordy, lordy, child, but you've grown a little and have even gotten more beautiful. Lo and behold, though your poor dead mother was a real pretty woman, you gonna have her beat by a country mile!"

And Delia hugged and kissed Amanda back into her large, capacious bosom.

"You don't know, hon, you don't know all the tears I cried and cried for your poor Moma killed by that no good, skunk Ted, and he takes advantage of you, having you put that makeup on and doll up like your Moma! I knew what was in that old skunk's head! And to top it all off, he robs you of your innocence and then tries to kill you, too, like he killed your Moma. Probably he'd put you in the same lime-covered grave like he did her. The police didn't want you to do it, but they asked me to identify your mother's remains. What there was left of them that poor woman was mostly bones from that there lime. Oh, I do hope Ted's burning in hell! After I find out for certain what he did to your poor Ma and tried to do to you, Lord, I swear I would have killed him myself, Yes, the Lord forgive me cause I's a Christian woman, but I'd have take a big sharp knife to him and just kept on cutting until that nasty pig of a man was just little old bits and pieces, I would have, I would have, too! 'Cause you's my baby pure and simple!"

Amanda kissed Delia fervently and said to her, in an effort to calm a very upset Delia, "I know so well, Delia, you do love me, but please, please no longer talk about my poor mother and how rotten

Ted was. I took care of him when it was my life or his and I think if there is a hell, he's in it. Now, let's leave it up to God, Delia, OK? We have a new and wonderful life to look forward to now!"

And Delia only hugged her more fiercely, the tears falling from her gleaming big black eyes, as if holding and hugging her and kissing her could erase all the evil and horror that had befallen her.

"You's my baby. When your mother came back from the hospital, she just up and dropped you in my lap and says, 'Delia, here, you take care of this baby. I don't know anything about babies!' I said to her, 'But this is your own little baby, Mam. Any natural woman know how to take care of her own baby!' Well, this woman doesn't and I don't want her interfering with my social life, Delia. I'll gladly pay you extra, but she's your responsibility, understand?' And then she was out the door with a rough, good-looking young man. You know how you Ma liked her men and all, well, you cried a little and looked at me with your big, big, innocent baby eyes, so blue and I hugged and kissed you and that was that."

Amanda hugged and kissed Delia again and said, "We both know how my mother was really no mother to me. You were my real mother, Delia and that's that! Now come on, Delia, Aunt Lavinia is dying to meet you in her mansion and take all three of us to Renards in Richmond. She told me it's a real fancy restaurant. Come on, Delia, let's go!"

"But, honey, I's never been driven in a limo before, like I's some rich, rich white lady and all never—"

"Come on, Delia, it's fun! It's a lot better than a taxi where you have to pay. And Vincent, the chauffeur is a good drive and I think he's very nice too. Come on, there's lots more I have to tell you before you meet my Great-Aunt Lavinia!"

Delia was led by Amanda down the rickety front steps down to the opened limo Delia's eyes grew big and round as Amanda assisted her into the back seat of the limo and then sat next to her.

Amanda then said to Vincent, "Vincent, this here's Delia."

And in his clipped British accent, Vincent had been chauffeuring Lords and Peers to Buckingham Palace and back, but Vincent had been very young then. He'd met and married a beautiful American girl and upon her tender admonitions, thought he'd try his luck in America. Aunt Lavinia had been driven by Vincent once and bribed and charmed him into working as her personal chauffeur. He'd been with Madame many years now.

Delia was mesmerized looking out of her window as the slabs and decrepit grayness of the slummy Bourbonville area peeled away and the clean lines and historic vistas of Richmond emerged into view.

Amanda hurriedly said to Delia, "Delia, don't get nervous when you meet Aunt Lavinia. She's strict with me, but she's so good. She's been so good to me and just wants so to make a little lady out of me. Why, she's even spoken of giving me a Debutante Ball when I turn eighteen. And she's even said if I do real well in school, she'll pay my full college tuition!"

Delia took this all in and said, smiling, "I was always hoping one of your better-off relatives or cousins would take you away from your mother for your own good and raise you in a good, Christian home."

Amanda smiled and said, "Oh, Aunt Lavinia is a good Christian and all. She's a really strict Roman Catholic and all. I suppose most of my relatives are. But believe me, she won't take offense at your being Southern Baptist and all. I really think once she gets to know you, she'll really like you, Delia. What I'm trying to say, Delia, is my secret plan in having you visit me and meeting Aunt Lavinia, I'm hoping she'll hire you full-time and you can be my personal Lady's Maid and all."

"I don't know, honey. I's done lived here most of my life. I'm used to it."

Amanda suddenly squeezed Delia's hand and said, "Oh, come on, Delia, I hate to say it, but you live in Bourbonville, the most dangerous slum in Richmond! Every summer there are break-ins, robberies, rapes, and murders! Aunt Lavinia's house is a magnificent mansion, believe me, and I don't have just one room, my bedroom like I did at Mother's house. I have a whole suite of rooms all to myself. You could take the bedroom off mine in my suite. I'm sure Aunt Lavinia would like that. That way you could watch me day and night."

Delia looked at her wide-eyed and said in a no-nonsense tone of voice, "Now why would this here Aunt Lavinia want you watched both day and night? Now tell me straight up, please. You haven't been carrying on with a young man or something which would cause your Aunt Lavinia grief, have you? Remember what I's done told you and told you how you have to love the Lord and be good and honorable, not like your poor, dead mother now!"

Amanda suddenly flushed and blushed to her roots and said, "Oh no, Delia, I don't have a boyfriend or anything like that. It's just that I sometimes dream of a really handsome Confederate soldier. I guess I was moaning in my sleep or something. Aunt Lavinia whipped me for it. Though she's promised never to do that again. Otherwise, I would ask the courts for a different legal guardian!"

"So she whipped you jus for having a naughty dream like most teenage girls have. Hell, that's jus theirs hormones playing games wid them like all natural things. That's strange and too strict. Anyways I hope she'll be sending you to school soon so you can develop friendships with boys and gals your own age! That would be healthy! Now I don't hold with no whippin' either. Mosts I ever did to you when you were real naughty and wouldn't eat the fine food I cooked for you was jus' spank you and sending you to bed in your room."

"Remember I's always put the meal on your tray and left it outside your bedroom so you'd eat it later. And your Ma said I could spank you when you were too fresh. But remember I hardly ever spanked you, 'cause I loved you too much to hurt you. But you know dreams can be more than dreams. Sometimes, dead folk who has no more business in the land of the living visit people in their dreams!"

Suddenly blushing furiously, "I don't want to talk anymore about it, Delia! Let's just keep this our little secret, OK?"

Delia looked at her stone-eyed again and said, "OK, Missy, OK. But I'm telling you, you's almost a woman grown now, and if I sees something funny or wrong, I'm going to do something about it!"

"Let's not talk about it anymore, Delia, please!"

"Of course, many, of course. I love ya, honey, I loves you and I loves the Lord too!"

Suddenly, before Amanda knew it, the limo was driving in the broad driveway into Aunt Lavinia's three-decker neoclassical mansion. The sun was still shining and the various beautiful flowers from the front garden beds were wavering in the winds and infusing the air with very fragrant natural perfumes. The servants, including Rita and Margaret immediately walked out of the front door and Billy O'Rourke, one of the male staff, offered the take the small black suitcase Delia had carried with her into the limo.

Rita smiled at Amanda and Delia and said, "The mistress is waiting for you in the den, Amanda and your friend."

Amanda said to Rita and for all the staff's benefit, "This woman, Delia Jackson, is far more than just a friend of mine. From infancy, she raised me and loved me better and more, far more than my own late mother did!"

Rita smiled at her and said, "We gathered as much, Amanda, now please follow us into the den!"

Proceeding into the luxurious den with its white ceiling and dark polished tables and deep-carpeted floors, Aunt Lavinia was sitting on her favorite deep-cushioned chair. Upon their entrance, she sat up and got out of the chair to greet Amanda and Delia. She kissed Amanda tenderly on the cheek and shook hands warmly with Delia.

"Well, I hope your trip out of Bourbonville was safe and uneventful. Vincent is an expert driver, I'm sure."

"Oh, we were safe, Vincent seemed to know the roads like the back of his hand, all right."

Suddenly, looking at Delia as if looking at her minutely, "And so, you are Delia, Delia Jackson, I believe."

Perking up, Delia said, "Yes, I am, ma'am. I took care of Amanda since she was first born after all. Yes, ma'am, the day her mother came back from the hospital with her. Why, she jus laid that po little baby on my lap and told me I was to raise her. Then Miss Aurelia went off a-galavanting on the arm of some good-looking, rough young piece of white trash man. Well, we knows her ways, Lord forgive her po soul. Then I looked at that helpless, po little baby, kissed her soft, sweet-smelling face and I says to both her and me and God. 'You ain't got no mommy really, nor no Daddy to love you and raise ya but you has got me, baby, you has got me.' And I promise you and God, I'll raise you right and love you, po little baby all alone, I'lls raise you right, baby!, I'll love you and raise you right!'"

Aunt Lavinia smiled at Delia in genuine affection and admiration. She said to both Amanda and Delia, "That's right. That's good and proper. When I was a baby and child, I had a black Mammy named Lucille. Oh, I loved her so and she loved me. As far as I was concerned, Delia, she was my real mother. Many years later, when I was middle-aged and she died, I had her buried with a beautiful headstone right near my family plot in the Eternal Rest Cemetery. Oh, my family and friends were fit to be tied, but I didn't care. Sometimes, I still cry for Lucille. Now tell me, Delia, do you love Amanda so much that if she were in mortal danger, real danger, you would move heaven and earth to protect her, if necessary, to die for her!"

"Any right-in-the-head natural mother who deserves the name would do that for her child, ma'am, and I certainly would for Amanda. I loves her like she was my own child. I has loved her like that since that day when her Ma plopped her in my big lap and then took off with some lover or other. Yes, if I has to I dies for her, yes, indeed, ma'am, yes indeed. But that don't mean I ever put up with her being naughty! Sometimes, I had to spank her when she was little to make her behave. I hates doing that, but sometimes she don't listen and I always warned her not to become like her own real mother. To be a far greater person than that!"

Aunt Lavinia smiled beatifically at Delia and Amanda and reached over and kissed Delia on her plump cheek and said, "Well, welcome aboard, Miss Delia, I offer you a permanent position here in my house. To be Amanda's personal maid. You'll live here near Amanda. I think you'll find the salary high and I pay for the health-care and medical and dental insurance of all my employees. Now let us have dinner at that wonderful chic restaurant in Richmond."

Delia visibly cried tears of joy and said to Lavinia, "I would have to stay here and work for you just to be with Amanda. My heart broken when I couldn't see her, and yes, my money is nearly all gone. Seems no one wants to hire a fat black cook and maidservant from a house where there has been murder, no matter how innocent I wus. Now I has a good a good job and I'll be vnear Amanda!, God, through you, Miss Lavinia has answered my prayers and may God bless you mighty much for doing this, Miss Lavinia."

Amanda went over to Aunt Lavinia and kissed her in the beginnings of a genuine love and said, "Thank you for this, Aunt Lavinia, thank you so much!"

Aunt Lavinia said, "Well now, let us go out to the Rendezvous restaurant."

Within minutes, they were in the limo being driven gladly to the beautiful parts of Richmond. All three women s transactions. Though the waiters and staff seemed momentarily shocked at seeing Delia's fat, black, and beautiful face following Aunt Lavinia and Amanda into the restaurant, but seeing Aunt Lavinia smile at them and saying a little loudly, "I want my usual seat and for my great niece and my new, ah, friend too if you please."

The head waiter smiled back and showed them to a broad, black table with an immaculately white lush tablecloth with a crystal vase full of scented white and red roses. They had a wonderful view of the fountain splashing on the very green yard where some well-dressed people sat with their gleaming glasses of drinks.

As expected and promised, the food was wonderful, and Delia was taken aback and impressed at being served herself for once.

The dessert of chocolate mousse was very, very delicious with luscious white cream topping. The ride home was wonderful with Amanda resting in Delia's arms. But to Amanda's disappointment, Delia insisted on going back to her home to make certain arrangements for her moving into Aunt Lavinia's home as a permanent staff. It would take two days, then they would send Vincent to get her.

Aunt Lavinia said she understood and gave her some money to settle some of her rent and other debts and to buy whatever else she thought necessary for her new life with her and Amanda. As Amanda was waving goodbye to Delia as she was being driven away, to her right, she saw the air suddenly sparkling and Lily, now her favorite spirit as well as an ancestress, dressed in her flowing black gown.

After Lily had materialized, she just whispered softly into Amanda's ear, "Expect some company tonight, Amanda. William is wanting to meet you again. Renew the acquaintance as it is."

Amanda said softly to Lily so that no other could hear her, "I don't know, Lily, with how Aunt Lavinia feels, and now Delia is coming to live here too, and I don't want to upset either of them."

Lily laughed lightly at her and said in a tone of tinkling temple bells, "Oh, come now, Mandy, you love this William, don't you? Try not to get caught this time, that's all. Follow your heart, girl! Follow your heart!"

Then Lily disappeared and Amanda knew William would come tonight and make that wonderful love to her. And she was beginning to love him, it was true what Lily had teasingly said to her. But really, William was just as much a ghost as Lily. What point was there in loving a ghost lover?

But he was so handsome and made such wonderful, wonderful love. Loving a living man psychologically didn't even compare. At least, she didn't have to worry about getting pregnant by him. If she could just hide the liaison, who was she hurting? Maybe this was one of the only ways this William felt physically alive again was through her. Certainly, the orgasms he gave her were very real and physical in intensity. Oh, why not?

Late that night, as Amanda was asleep, she found herself in an intense dream. She saw William before her, he was completely naked. Oh, so, so handsome with his nice built and sturdy, hairy legs. In her dream, they were in a sunlit cottage and she was in a very soft bed. But she thought, *What am I getting into? He's a ghost, for Christ's sake, a spirit, and I'm starting regular school next week!*

But almost against her will, she opened her arms to him and he came to her bed in all his brawny beauty. They kissed intensely, and it sent those fiery, delicious tingles through her. Oh, he was so, so handsome, much more so than her dead stepfather, Ted. He began moaning to her, "I love you, Katey, I love you and never want to be separate from you again!"

She stopped kissing him, looked at him sternly, and said admonishingly, "Hey, William, I'm not this Katey! I'm Amanda now!"

"But a long time ago, you were my Katey!"

"Well, whatever you say, Wiliiam, and she began returning his hot, fervid kisses. Waves of sheer ecstasy shot through her in fiery tingles. When he entered her, the erotic intensity built and built in her until she climaxed against his white marble-hard body. William's hoarse breathing signaled his explosion in her and he said, "Sweet Jesus in heaven," hoarsely and then sighed."

Then she awoke and it was the early beginnings of dawn and William was there with her in her bed and felt very physical to her as she lay back and let him continue caressing and kissing her all over.

For a ghost, he felt so real, so physical. This was so, so wonderful indeed! As near as she could make out, it was still predawn, so no one was up about in the house. But she had enough presence of mind to say to William, "William, very soon, you'll have to be more careful about seeing me and making love to me. In a few days, Delia will come as my personal maid and she doesn't hold with no ghost stuff, especially with my being lovers with one! We'll both have to be more careful!"

"Why are you so worried about an old black Mammy! I can handle her!"

"No, William, no! If you love me, don't ever frighten her or hurt her. I love her!"

"All right! I won't harm her, but why are you carrying on so about an old nigger wench, anyway? When I was alive on earth, if a nigger slave didn't mind his or her place, one just whipped them good and proper! They learned their place all right mighty quick!"

Amanda became very angry. "William, this is a very different time and place from your time. First, don't ever use that awful term for black people in my presence, period. It's wrong, it's derogatory, and I won't have it, period! I love Delia like a mother or grandmother. She's the one who really raised me! You even try to harm her and I'll have nothing to do with you, and I'll use whatever powers of being a part-witch to really hurt and banish you from here for all time! Understand?"

"Oh, chickenshit, why all this fuss over one old nigra gal?"

Then William completely disappeared from her bed, and Amanda was not altogether sorry to see him go. She knew he came from a very different time and place and had probably been very much in favor of slavery! Well, she would just wait and see what happened!

In a way, she was looking forward to Delia coming to the house and her starting school soon. Yes, she thought she'd experienced ecstasy with William, but really, as she had previously thought, what kind of future, romantic, and otherwise, did she have with a ghost lover? She did not particularly wish to wind up like the Aunt Eliza, Aunt Lavinia's younger sister! No, really, the land of the living offered a lot more in terms of relationships and normal, healthy living!

The next Wednesday, Delia was going to come with Aunt Lavinia paying for the moving truck to bring her belongings to the mansion. Vincent was going out around 10 A.M. and going to pick up Delia. Amanda couldn't wait to see her again!

Having breakfast and later lunch with Aunt Lavinia, Aunt Lavinia had said that she, Amanda, must acquaint Delia with the ways and rules of the house. She really expected her live-in staff and everyone else to have said their prayers and have gone to bed by then. When Delia came, she herself would tell her her duties which would be mostly to her, Amanda.

She was to help her get up at 7:00 A.M., help her dress, after she'd brushed her teeth and showered and get her ready for school. They would both have breakfast together with her and the staff in the dining room. Then, at 8:30 A.M., she, Amanda, would be driven by Vincent to school. As to her day and evening duties to Amanda, when Amanda was off in school, she was to clean her own and Amanda's suite of rooms, clean, dust, swab, vacuum so that everything was immaculate and spotless for Amanda when Vincent brought her back from school.

If Delia, during that time, ran out of things to do she could see her, Aunt Lavinia and they could talk together and even pray together. Their being of different faiths really didn't matter at all. They were both Christians and religiously inclined and that was really all that mattered in Aunt Lavinia's mind. Aunt Lavinia had found Delia singularly pleasant, and she always prayed both morning and evening and fancied her company when she prayed.

Amanda told her that unfortunately, Delia had some trouble reading, but always, daily when she wasn't too busy, prayed from her Bible in her room, and had tried to teach Amanda stories and parables from the Bible.

"She sounds like truly a godly, Christian woman, Amanda. And I'm so glad, going to that school with both boys and girls together, coming from the home that you did, you will need all the good, Christian upbringing you can get. I, of course, will do you my best in that department, but it's good you will have this Delia here, whom you so clearly love and respect to guide you in righteous living too."

"You know, I think that the only reason Delia stayed on as my mother's maid, cleaner, and cook was, really, because of me. Oh, don't get me wrong, Delia needed the job and all, but being such a good domestic and cook that she is, she could have had a good-paying job with any other prosperous white family anywhere in the state. I could tell that Delia had long lost any caring and respect for my mother and her crazy lifestyle. Sometimes, my mother yelled at her over nothing, really, and I saw her secretly crying over it. No, the only reason I think Delia stayed in that house was to love and raise me as best she could give the way my mother lived and all. I think you'll find Delia as good and faithful as she is nice. Thank you so much for providing employment to Delia here, Aunt Lavinia."

With that, Aunt Lavinia bent toward her at the table and kissed her on her cheek. Shaking her head a little, Aunt Lavinia said to her, "Sometimes, Amanda, please don't tell a soul, but I'm a little bit of a witch. I kind of have the second sight. I can tell things about people. And after I actually met her, I could tell Delia was like my Mammy Lucille, strong and good and so, so kind. And because, too, I think Lucille would have died for me, I think your Delia would die for you. Honey, too, we were both very lucky to have such women in our lives. It doesn't matter to me or you that they are of a different race. What matters is that they both loved us so, especially in our time of need. If this Delia hadn't been in your mother's employ when you were born, you might not have survived infancy, the way your mother, my daughter was, really. And that's just plain facts. Now, for this immense favor to you, and I'm glad I did it for you, you must do me a great favor in return."

"Whatever it is, I'll do, Aunt Lavinia," Amanda said.

"That next week, you will really apply yourself well at school. And you will conduct yourself properly at all times to be a credit to myself and what decency remains in our family. All right, that's all I ask of you, darling."

Amanda placed her hand on her heart and said, "I swear I will do my best, Aunt Lavinia, for both you and Delia!"

"All right then! Now that we understand each other, child, why don't you go out into the gardens and pick me some of our beautiful roses for your Delia's rooms. That should cheer her up somewhat."

"Gladly, Aunt Lavinia, I know what color roses she likes best, too."

Later that day, the rooms that were to be used by Delia soon were nicely decorated with lovely white, pink, and red roses in crystal vases with fresh water with a little sugar to make them last longer. She knew Delia would love them. Back a while, when they had lived with her mother and Ted, there were some neglected rose bushes in their backyard. Sometimes, in summer, Delia would go out and pick some roses for the family's dining table and have a few in her own room too.

Amanda so wanted Delia to like her stay with them. That night, though, she dreamt she was in a field with large rambling wild roses and other flowers. It was a cool but sunny day, and she was dressed in a dress from a different period. Why, she thought, she was wearing a dress like this Katey, William's old girlfriend during the Civil War. In another second, she saw William's handsome face and felt his strong, enfolding arms about her.

Before she knew it, she was naked and so was William on the lush green ground beneath some bushes. The nude William was kissing and embracing her and kissing her so heatedly and expertly. She loved his musculature and hard, hairy body. Delicious, erotic tingles coursed throughout her body, and she was kissing back all over. When he finally entered her, waves of orgasmic ecstasy rippled through her and she moaned in her rapture long and hard.

"Katey, Katey, Katey!" William moaned in his own rapture above her as her fingernails raked his back. Then the settings changed and she was in her own muffled bed in what looked like the predawn hours. William, naked, was there with her moaning softly. She instinctively nibbled his ear and said to him, "William, you must remember whoever I was to you before, I'm not Katey whoever she was! I'm Amanda now!"

"But you were having a dream as my fiancée, Katey, and so you were Katey a long time ago. She and I were to marry soon after the war. I think the last time we were together, she became pregnant and I got killed at Gettysburg. A little later, she died of influenza or some such disease back then. Then, I'm positive she came back as you."

Then Amanda realized that it was just about dawn. Knowing that her William was to vanish completely very soon into the nothingness from which he'd come, she grabbed him and said to him, "William, I think I really, really love you. But Delia's coming here tomorrow, and please only see me when she is very deeply asleep. She'll be sleeping in the room adjoining mine. And she wouldn't take to you at all. She's like Aunt Lavinia in that way. They don't approve of love-making outside of marriage and especially not with a ghost! No, that would be something evil and twisted to them!"

"Goddamn it, Amanda-Katey, why all this fuss over an old, old lady who forgot about love and pleasure a long, long time ago and how magic it can be. And what gets me really mad is why the fuss about a nigra servant girl! In my time, the nigras knew their place! That's one of the reasons the North and South fought and I was killed. To keep niggers in their place!"

Amanda went white with anger and shock and said, "I won't have you speaking badly of Aunt Lavinia and Delia! They're like real mothers to me! Delia really raised me and all, and I hate those hateful terms you use to describe her and her race! Only cruel, stupid, classless, and nasty people say those slurs about them today! Begone from me until you learn some real discretion and more kindness to others who aren't white!"

William looked furiously at her, and little alarm bells went off in Amanda's head. Well she knew how physically strong and rugged even William's ghost was. If he were really that mad at her, he could always just strangle her or something and then just vanish into thin air and not get caught or punished except possibly by God with the sin of her murder on his hands! She knew now she was indeed playing a very dangerous game Just before she yelled to William to vanish and never see her again, he yelled at her, "Bitch, whore! This isn't over between us!" and vanished into thin air.

A white-faced maid, Rita, looking startled from a sound sleep suddenly opened her door and turned on the lights.

She said to Amanda, fear on her face, "I heard loud voices in this room! I heard a man's loud voice screaming at you!"

"As you can see, Rita, there's no one else in here with me, now go and let me get at least some more sleep!"

Looking strangely at Amanda, she said, "The only type of man who can vanish suddenly into thin air is not a living one! You been consorting with ghosts again, Amanda? You know your Aunt Lavinia won't have that!"

Sitting erect in bed, very white with anger herself, she spat at Rita, "Who I have or who I speak to in this room, there is no one alive with me, is there? Now, you found out what the so-called dead can do the time Aunt Lavinia whipped me and someone invisible protected me, didn't you and Margaret both! You bring any tales of this to Aunt Lavinia's ears to needlessly upset her, you will indeed find out how viciously physical, even murderous, angry ghosts can be! Now get out of here, Rita, and bother me no more!"

Rita's face went white herself with fear and panic as she instantly realized she was now dealing with a totally preternatural force from which there was absolutely no defense she could call on, and she hurriedly closed the door and ran down the corridor and stairs to the safety of her own bedroom with the still-sleeping Margaret.

Amanda felt kind of bad about using that kind of threat to Rita, but if the fool girl told Aunt Lavinia about her and William, he probably would kill the stupid interfering maid as well as possibly her obstreperous Aunt Lavinia.

Well, much as she now disliked William, she did not want Rita interfering in any way with her life. And tomorrow, Delia would come to the house to be with her; she said a little prayer to God and went to sleep, a deep and now dreamless sleep! The next day, in the afternoon as Delia, with her suitcases and belongings were brought in, Amanda fell furiously alive into Delia's arms, kissing her as if she hadn't seen her in a hundred years. She was so happy, rapturously happy to see Delia. The thought that Delia was to be there, her constant companion and personal maid, was like being transported to heaven to her! She was in ecstasy!

Aunt Lavinia very warmly welcomed Delia into her house, too, with a little kiss on her cheek. She said, all smiles, "I know how much you both really love each other and I know how devoted you are and will be to Amanda, Delia. I want her protected by strong love and devotion like yours and mine, always. With her heritage in mind, she'll need good, godly people around her, always guiding and teaching and protecting her!"

Delia looked straight at Aunt Lavinia and said, "I knows, Mam, Lord God how I know that! In the other house, with her late mother behaving like she did, I's tried, I's tried so to protect her, my little baby always from bad stuff there, but it wasn't always easy!" Then she kissed Amanda again on the mouth and she said to her, "Please forgive me, Mandy, for leaving you all alone with your stepfather that night and his dressing you like a little doll in you dead mother's dress and jewels! I's had a real bad feeling about the whole thing! I thought of calling the police, but they would've jus laughed at me, a fat black cook and maid trying to interfere in white folks' business. But I cried and prayed for you all that night! Well, he had his way with you, but you kilt him before he could've kilt you! Thank the Lord!"

"And what I prayed for for whole years has happened! A wonderful, godly relative of yours has taken you in and will educate you and love you and make a fine Christian lady out of you! I prayed for you so hard on my hurting knees, darling! Well, enough now with this chat and carrying on, now! Show me to my room now with my things and explain to me with my duties to me, Miss Lavinia, and the Lord's sweet and blessed thanks to you, Miss Lavinia, for taking in my little darling girl like you done, I'll be the best maid you ever had. I'm mighty beholding to you, Miss Lavinia, for saving my precious, pretty little babe, Mandy, when so much has happened to her!"

And with that, Mandy led Delia to her suite of rooms and showed her her big room and fancy bed and furniture of her very own.

A few hours later, after Delia had been helped to settle in by Rita and Margaret who both seemed to like Delia almost immediately, Delia was sitting in a large pink satin chair in Amanda's room. Amanda was sitting on her bed near her. Both women were together alone and drinking some delicious cups of tea. Amanda found that with Delia ensconced in the mansion and back in her life, she could not be more happy.

Then Delia's large black eyes bored directly into her and she said, "Darling, I have to talk to you about something serious."

A funny, nervous queasiness percolating in her stomach, Amanda put her teacup down and asked, "What is it, Delia? Don't you think you'll be happy here?"

Delia frowned at her and said, "I be right worried about you, Mandy! I think, I knos you can see and hear a lot more than most folks. Ya got the second sight and some people in yo family have it, some don't, but I knows ya got it strong! Well, I has it, too if ya wants to know the truth. Ma granny, ma ma' ma was one of those Cajun conjure women from the Louisiana Delta. Oh, she could see the spirits and wid them herbs and such she helped cure the sick. Well, ever since I wus little I sees the spooks, too, and I knows things that has yet to take place."

"Is that why when I was little, you always warned me about the cellar and the ghosts of those poor slaves there!"

"Yes, them spirits there hates white folks because of what happened to them there. But ya found that out on ya own, didn't ya?"

"Indeed I did, Delia, indeed I did!"

"Well, I think, in fact in my heart, I knows you be dreaming of a long-dead man! I think ya might even love him! Listen, it's dangerous to be mixing the two worlds, the living and the dead! Ya's supposed to pray for the dead, to help them move into the light of heaven. Please, honey, darling, ya got a good situation here! Ya Aunt Lavinia loves you heart and soul! Soon you'll be goin to a nice school. There, you's gonna meet boys and girls ya own age. What I says is pray for the dead! And move them out of ya life! The lost dead can be trapped in the land of the living until they're forced to and they can mess up the lives of the living who out of love or whatever, holds them here! Let this man go, Amanda! Start a whole new life here, a clean, fresh new start! OK, honey child?"

Amanda frowned to herself. In spite of her knowing that this William was both very strong and could be dangerous, she was so attracted to him; she didn't really want to let him go. At least not completely from her life.

She said to Delia, "Of course, Delia, of course, I understand. Come on, want to see the new dresses Aunt Lavinia has bought for me and my going to school?"

But all the time that evening, she was thinking of William. He was so handsome and such a good lover, she definitely didn't want him out of her life. She acknowledged to herself, his personality had its rough spots. Like his racial prejudice and bigotry against blacks and probably other non-whites. Well, he was a frigging Confederate officer who'd been killed fighting for the cause of the South and its revolting slavery and other prejudices. Of course, he'd have the attitudes of his time and place.

But as long as she understood where and in what capacity she was coming from, she felt she could handle him, as revolting as his racial views were to her. He really may have been bigoted poison, but it came in such a pretty, virile package, why throw the baby out with the bathwater? It wasn't as if she really thought they could one day marry and live forever and ever as happy husband and wife in some ethereal of both the living and the earthbound dead. No such place existed on the earth or, as far as she knew, anyplace else in heaven or hell.

She knew Delia was right, the living and the dead were two separate entities, never to be conjoined as lovers. But William was so, so handsome. Her blood ran wild with desire just hearing his deep, melodious voice, saw his devastatingly handsome face and form. Why, in her right mind, should she give him up just to satisfy Delia and Aunt Lavinia and their more prudish outlooks?

Her stepfather had taught her passion well. She knew that like her mother, she was a highly sensual and highly sexed young woman. She was probably born that way. As long as she was halfway discreet and could somehow force William to be, too, why couldn't she have her cake and eat it too?

That night, before school was to begin, she began to dream as she thought she would, she was the girl Katey again in her blue dress walking alone in some farm fields she recognized as belonging to Katey's family. Maybe it was as William had told her, a past life, maybe it was just a fantasy on her part. Then, all of a sudden, there was William dressed in his gray Confederate officer's uniform and looking so, so handsome.

Without a single thought, she breathlessly ran into his strong arms and they were kissing wildly and touching each other everywhere. Then, before she even knew it, they were both completely naked and interlocked in mad, rapturous embraces. She loved his hard, red lips kissing her everywhere imaginable. She loved his strong, strong embraces, his fevered kisses, his hard, beautiful hairy chest and legs.

She was in erotic ecstasy now and did what she had sworn to herself she would not do again for discretion's sake in the dangerous would she was still very much a part of.

She moaned aloud, the ecstasy she felt in her coupled loins, the very fire in her veins. She moaned and moaned and raked William's naked back with her long manicured nails. And then, in less than a second, she felt hands pulling her, pulling her out from under William's all so penetrating and covering hot male body.

She began screaming aloud and then being slapped in the face, she suddenly opened her eyes and saw an angry and frightened-looking Delia who was grappling her with both hands roughly and then taking out a wooden cross as Amanda also saw that her lover William was there with her on her bed as naked as he was in her interrupted dream and looking startled and very enraged at Delia.

Delia pulled her suddenly away from William completely and stood up to a now bellowing William with her cross which looked like an old relic.

"You black, interfering nigger wench! I'll kill you for interfering with me and my eternal love!"

"She's not your love! You's a dead man, a goddamn ghost for Christsakes, a ghost! Amanda, couldn't you do better than this here ghost-man who must have forgot he's dead! Listen here, you ghost! Go back, I says, go back to the heaven or hell you belong to! The living and the dead cannot in the Lord's name mingle! Go back now! Leave my baby alone!"

And so saying, she fearlessly lunged at William with the wooden cross and began mumbling some French-Cajun words at him. Amanda realized it was probably some Cajun spell Delia had learned from her Cajun granny to dispel and combat ghosts. William's solid-looking body began to waver and become transparent with the utterance of the magic words.

Then William yelled aloud, "No," and solidified as if by force of will and jumped at Delia and held her down on the bed and began strangling her. Delia was gasping for breath and beginning to turn blue when Amanda suddenly shouted, "William, no! I say no."

With Delia getting herself killed for her, she made up her mind that William must go from her forever! Suddenly totally infuriated at him, she felt a force she'd never before realized she had! It came from the gypsy-witch she was from so long ago and the other witches in her lineage. Nothing and no one must ever harm Delia.

A fiery white light came from her outstretched hands and completely enveloped William He suddenly looked at Mandy and screamed at her, "No, baby, no!" And then enveloped completely in the burning light, he totally vanished and Amanda screamed at him, "I banish you away from me or anyone else you can still harm, forever, William, go, go, go! Go back to where you came from I say, go back now!"

And then the room's light switch was turned on and a startled-looking Aunt Lavinia, her eyes nearly popping out of her head, looked at Amanda and the light-engulfed vanishing William and the still-gasping Delia on the bed!

When William had totally vanished with the devouring light, she screamed at Amanda in anger and terror, "What in heaven's name is the meaning of this?"

Amanda went down on her bed and hugged Delia and quickly kissed her and, tears streaming down her face, she said to Aunt Lavinia who was surrounded by her maids, Rita and Margaret, "I have some explaining to you, Aunt Lavinia!"

"Indeed you do, though I can surmise what this is all about!"

After dressing, Amanda got up and, alone with Aunt Lavinia and a now recovered Delia, began telling her aunt the full story of her involvement with this William. She was crying because she feared her great-aunt would now disown her and also crying that she could never see William again whom, despite his grave faults, she had so foolishly loved beyond all reason.

Long into the night and into the early morning hours, Amanda carefully explained about her seeing ghosts from the time she was a toddler on.

She also explained even the truth of her and Ted and how, as if helpless to her own overriding passion, she'd made love with Ted even near her mother's uncovered skeletal remains. How she felt she was like her mother, overwhelmed with raw physical desire. She told her aunt about the ghost Lily and what Lily had told her about the royal foundation of their line and how, often, the descendants had way too much eroticism for their own good. She also explained about the magical powers they often had, too.

Her Aunt Lavinia trembled and cried in both pity and horror, too. But she well knew Amanda was telling the truth, the complete truth. This was her secret granddaughter, after all. Then Amanda explained about meeting William through Lily and how she was instantly attracted to him because he was so, so handsome and resembled Ted.

Her aunt said, "So he was the ghost who struck me and my maids when I was whipping you for your own good!"

Amanda nodded and said, "Yes, he protected me, and he should have because that whipping was wrong! If you had kept your baby, my mother, you too would have probably whipped her for her having too much sensuality and passion! Don't you get it, Aunt Lavinia, however wrong you think it, it's just how some poor people in this family are born!"

And Amanda flung herself down on her bed which she'd been standing beside and began crying miserably, with Delia stroking her hair and trying to comfort her.

"Wherever you go, Amanda, I's going, too. Someone gots to protect and I'm it and your Aunt Lavinia knew it."

"My, my, my! A pretty sight you both make. The new heiress and her beloved maid."

They hadn't realized that Aunt Eliza had crept up on them from the middle of the parlor!

"Aunt Eliza, sorry about your not getting anything in the will. But honestly, there was little love lost between Aunt Lavinia and you!"

"Come on, I didn't really expect anything in Lavinia's will. Besides that, though I've never lived as well as Lavinia, I probably have ten times the money she ever did. If one is wise and has a certain sight, let us say, there's no telling how far stocks can grow. And mine have grown exceeding well indeed."

"With a little help from spirit friends, no doubt, Aunt Eliza. But I want to tell you, Aunt Lavinia was richer than you in one thing and it's what really counts. She had love and sweetness in her heart. That's why she claimed me as she did and took me in, love. You had a chance to adopt me too, but you passed on that."

"Oh, Amanda, come on. The way I live in my mansion in Gettysburg, you wouldn't have liked it one bit. I knew Lavinia would claim you for her own by your secret blood-tie and groom you to be a proper lady, which she did, didn't she? But you know, I don't care what she did with her money, who she left it to, in her will, she didn't mention me at all, her own sister! I can't say it doesn't hurt, but I lived a life she found, ah, objectional, I suppose."

Amanda then jumped up from Delia and kissed the withered, wrinkled face of this formidable Aunt Eliza.

"But, Aunt Eliza, whatever your lifestyle, which I do find a bit odd and bizarre too, I've become very fond of you, really! I don't know if it's love yet, but we are family and you are always welcome in this place which is now truly all mine. Please come visit as often as you choose. You'll always be welcome here. There are some things I can still learn from you. Oh, by the way, Craig, out of the blue, called me yesterday and wants to see me tomorrow."

"Oh," said Aunt Eliza, "and does he have his parents' permission to come here and see you now?"

"That's just it. Apparently, word leaked out to the bluebloods around Richmond how much my inheritance would be, they've changed their attitude toward me a bit, including Craig's parents. I guess the incident at the cemetery is forgiven and forgotten in most quarters."

"My, my, how money always does sweeten a pot. So now you'll no longer be a pariah to them. There is one man who I suspect is still bitter to you, that judge who called you out at the burial. I know the sort of man he is. Never, and I repeat, never expect any quarter from that man. In fact, with the fact that you'll be so rich and hence powerful, he may stir up the rabble, oh, every city has them, against you to do you harm and drive you out if they can!"

Amanda frowned at her great aunt and said, "That man, a judge, would stoop to that?"

"Yes, I say he is a vile thoroughly nasty man. I wonder if there are any guns or even rifles here and some male servants who can use them!"

"There are indeed, there are indeed. Aunt Lavinia believed in being prepared for trouble, and she deliberately hired some male servants who could shoot. In fact, Aunt Eliza, I can load and fire both guns and rifles. Jeffers, one of our chefs, secretly taught me how to load and fire! Aunt Lavinia would have been horrified, but

I wanted to be protected at all times, After all, I shot my murderous stepfather to death when he tried to kill me years ago. I have a great respect for arms in dangerous situations. If Judge Withers starts trouble, he'll get trouble back!"

"Why," Aunt Eliza said, her green eyes crinkling and smiling, "it seems my great-niece is a regular Anne Oakley! Still, darling, there are other weapons besides guns and rifles. Deadlier and more frightful weapons I have at my disposal, and you, Amanda, now do yours."

Looking at both the old and young woman preparing for battle, Delia looked at them both round-eyed in shock, even horror, "Hold on there! Now! Guns and rifles can kill people and leave bodies and you two could go to jail, especially using them against this old, nasty but real powerful judge!"

"Dearie, Delia, just leave it to us. There'll be no killing, really, if trouble does come. Just a bunch of stupid, cowardly rabble and their judge will be in jail for their ill intent to us," said Aunt Eliza.

"Yes, Delia, those men will be getting the scare of their lives and they all deserve it. Still, I'll have the male servants with the guns and rifles in case it becomes necessary after all. But with Aunt Eliza helping us, no one will get killed, just scared the bejesus out of!"

With that, Amanda turned to face the lawyer whose rendition of Aunt Lavinia's will had made her so, so rich now, so awfully, extravagantly rich now. She thanked him, then left with Aunt Eliza and Delia in tow to plan for the trouble all three women felt would come that night.

Very late that night, a band of around twelve men dressed in white hoods and robes silently came to the front lawn of the Mannon estate. They took their wooden crosses out, throwing a little liquid gas on them, and lit them. The flames shot high into the air, the fiery light piercing the thick all-enveloping darkness, lit only by a full silver moon up in the sky.

They started shouting and shooting some rifles into the sky overhead and hooting and hollering!

"Come out of that house, you nigger-loving bitch, you disgrace to the county and city of Richmond! Get out of here now and leave town and never show your nigger-loving face around her again! We'll tar and feather you, you daughter of a slut and whore, you and your old witch of a crazy Aunt Eliza! We'll get that freak-show ghost-loving witch out of here too!"

All of a sudden, there was a quick movement from the low-lying trees and bushes. The little KKK band led, of course, by a drunken Judge Withers, were facing loaded rifles and guns from twelve male servants of the house they were threatening.

And a piercing, mocking young woman voice said to them, "Oh no, Judge Withers, we won't be going anywhere. Move one inch, and my friends here will shoot and so will I! As a matter of fact, we won't be going anywhere tonight, but you all will be, to jail for what you're attempting now, you racist KKK bastards! I was warned of this plot by a special friend! And I and these men, my loyal servants can very accurately fire and shoot! Here, I'll show you how!"

With that, Amanda hastily dressed in a nightgown and bathrobe with the rifle she was holding straight ahead of her like another bodily appendage. Her long aureole of gold hair glinted silver-gold in the moonlight. And then she fired and the shots hit the ground not three inches in front of the fat, rotund form of Judge Withers who looked totally ridiculous in that white KKK costume.

The judge pissed his pants and started screaming in rage, "So you can shoot, bitch! Me and my brothers of the Klan will still get you now and burn the mansion to the ground!"

Amanda looked at him and laughed aloud mockingly, "Want to tell your KKK friends around you you just pissed your fucking pants you big coward! I'll have you in jail and then I'll personally sue you for every cent you have. Your name will be shit in this city and state! It'll make national news, for Christ's sake trying to terrorize an innocent girl, her old aunt, and her servants. Don't worry, you won't die just yet! I have better weapons than rifles and guns! Here, William and your friends, get them!"

Then a piercing rebel yell came thundering out at the KKK and some translucent dark shadows materialized out of seemingly dark air and ran right at the now quivering forms of the judge and his KKK band.

Some of the ghostly figures were holding long translucent rifles with bayonets attached atop them and they began attacking and pummeling the scared-as-shit judge and the KKK. One of them ran up to the judge and hit him hard with the butt of his translucent ghostly rifle.

The judge screamed aloud in horror and then agony and passed out and fell unconscious to the ground.

The ghost band of rebel soldiers caught up with the fleeing forms of the KKK men and flailed them with their rifle butts, too, and even pierced their arms and legs with their ghostly bayonets.

Within minutes, the entire group of KKK would-be urban terrorists were either wounded unconscious on the ground or crying out in agony with their wounds and the sight of the ghost soldiers who'd attacked them.

Then, laughing gleefully, Amanda said to her Aunt Eliza who had bravely stood beside her hidden by a tree, "Now go into the house and call the cops while we still have them and those dingy white robes they're wearing!"

And then she turned to a wavering, translucent form that stood before her now and she said, "Thank you so much, William! You are my hero, you and your men. I'll see you later."

Amanda's armed male servants hadn't been expecting any help in the matter, from ghosts or otherwise, but, knowing they were now safe because they had helped Amanda and Aunt Eliza, hurried back to the mansion.

An amazed squadron of police vehicles came and, realizing the situation, called in some extra squad cars and some ambulances too. They hauled the wounded off to a nearby hospital and arrested the lot of them too. A mugshot of a white-gowned and battered Judge Withers appeared in the next day's edition of the *Richmond Chronicle.*

No one believed their stories about ghosts attacking them or Amanda and Aunt Eliza commanding such ghosts. Many people in the city were glad to see the backside of Judge Withers whom many felt for a long time was greedy and infinitely corrupt.

The judge lost his position immediately and, later on in a prison, was presented with the legal papers of a suit by Amanda and Aunt Eliza Mannon too. Not only would he be relieved of his judgeship, but he, as a result of the suit, would be penniless too.

When Amanda later heard of his eventual suicide in his disgrace, she only smiled. Revenge was a dish best served cold. While the good people of Richmond were still leery of Amanda, now there was some respect thrown in and not a little fear.

For every single KKK man in the group who had burned their little crosses on the deep lawn of the Mannon mansion had also done time in jail along with the judge. She would have sued them too, but they were, as Aunt Eliza had said, just white-trash rabble and had no real money to be extracted of.

What they did have were their marketable skills as mechanical or general laborers. But with the few years of hard prison-time they served with the judge, they found even meager employment where they lived even more difficult to obtain. Most of them crossed the line and became alcoholics and nicotine fiends and the moonshine they commonly consumed led to ugly divorces and early cirrhosis of the liver. Most died of it and cancer too.

With what had happened to their cohorts, other Klansmen really thought twice about harming the prominent Mannons of Richmond, Virginia, no matter how liberal Amanda was or caring about those damn niggers. To their minds, always to their minds a black, not matter how nice or even light, was just a goddamn nigger.

In fact, Amanda could have walked down Richmond's main street in broad daylight with a black man, and outside of some dirty looks, no one would have done or said anything. Amanda never did do that, ever, not because she was afraid to, but her world now revolved around her ghost-lover and protector, William, and her living lover, Craig Weston.

Her liaison with Craig had come about this way. Her Great-Aunt Eliza on her last night in the house before she left for her home in Gettysburg, Pennsylvania, Eliza had said to her.

"You know, you got real nonstop sex and passion with the so-called dead. I bet your lover William is quite a lover! The dead are hungry for the living! When they're with us, they have what they consider an orgasm, it's like they are alive again in passion's throes."

Amanda replied and, nodding to Eliza, said, "That may be, but you know I went steady with this boy, Craig Weston, all through high school. We came close to making love, but I obeyed my Aunt Lavinia's command about no sex before marriage. Sometimes I regret it."

"Oh, that silly wimp of a callow boy who let his mother slap him publicly at my sister's burial? And when he was supposed to see you again, got scared off by what you and I and the ghosts did to the Judge and his little KKK posse. You call him a man?"

"Well, Aunt Eliza, to the average person on the street in this city and anywhere, all this ghost-business is really scary, even horrific."

Her great-aunt suddenly grabbed her by the shoulders and began to shake her a little. For a withered old lady, Aunt Eliza was surprisingly strong.

"Well, then, go and find out for yourself what this Craig Weston is really like in bed! He's at that college now in Ohio. Call him, take a plane or whatever, and see him, make love to him and see, just see if he gives you one bit of the orgasmic pleasure that your William does. Go and see! William himself won't be too happy about it and so bind him to this house so he can't escape and try to kill your poor little Craig, the dear boy! Find out for yourself what losers in bed and in life living men are! OK?"

Amanda suddenly grabbed her great-aunt's claw-like hands off her shoulders and threw them back at the angry, wizened old lady. *The old witch,* she thought.

"Listen, you seem to forget, Aunt Eliza, with the living, one can marry, actually have children someday, and in spite of my ever-neglectful, nympho mother, I've always wanted a baby, boy or girl, it doesn't matter to me. A little baby I could give all the love my mother denied me as a baby and child growing up!"

"You want children now, do you?" Aunt Eliza leered at her sarcastically. "Children, like living men, are lechers and takers, too. Cute, possibly adorable, but takers and users who can and often do break a mother's heart more times than not. But maybe it's good you want children. Except for some scattered, distant cousins, we are the last of the Mannons. Yes, that's just what the world needs, more Mannon witches and mediums to the core."

"Aunt Eliza, look I'm going to bed tonight. You're leaving tomorrow and I'll contact Craig at his school and arrange a visit. I hope he still wants to see me after the trouble I've caused around here with this crazy Southern sensibility."

"Oh, don't worry, he'll see you. Why not? You're young, very beautiful, and now very rich. He'd be a fool not to see you and make love to you. After William, though, don't be surprised if he's just a big disappointment in both bed and in life too."

Amanda said a hasty good night. God, that old lady could be so irritating. She went upstairs to Delia's rooms near her own. She found Delia praying in her large feather-bed with a tattered Bible.

Delia's serious face suddenly beamed a smile of love up to her and said, "Sugar, how are you? Anything you want to talk over wid me, anything bothering you in particular?"

"Oh, Delia, just between us, Aunt Eliza can really get on one's nerves. She's a cynical, self-righteous old lady who prefers ghost lovers to living men and thinks I should do likewise."

"That old lady is a crazy old witch and I is glad she's leaving tomorrow. Hey, I knows you have that ghost William and you know how I feel about that. Whatever happened to that good-looking boy you so liked, Craig Weston?"

"Funny you should ask. Aunt Eliza was just speaking of him very badly. He's not a wimp or a Mama's boy, Delia. He's just sensitive I guess. Anyway, I'm going to call him at his college tomorrow and try to arrange a visit if I can!"

"That's good, honey. Stick with the living. That other stuff, the stuff your Aunt Eliza likes with the spirits, is crazy stuff and the Lord is against it! Let the dead rest!"

"Oh, Delia, that's just it, I think I love William too much to give him up. The way he makes me feel in bed! He drives me crazy with passion. The ecstasy is beyond belief."

"It's a sin, you know, a worse sin than your poor dead mother ever did. She kept herself with the living flesh only. She was a cheap, sinful woman who was a horrible mother to you. But at least what she did with men was normal, if too much. What you is doing with William is a whole different thing and could drive you out of your mind someday. Anyway, is that how you want to wind up a crazy, ghost-driven old lady like Aunt Eliza?"

"No, no, no, Delia, I don't want that, I swear! I want to marry someday and have children and love them totally. Even I know I can never have that with William."

"No, you can't! I'm glad you know that, Why not just banish this William back to Gettysburg where he came from, out of your life?"

"No, no, Delia! I can't do that, not now, not ever! Every time I see him I melt. Every time he materializes and touches me, I light on fire. His kisses and caresses and his making violent love to me are what I think of when he's not there and what I dream of at night as I lie asleep, usually besides him. In the morning before he again vanishes with the growing morning light, I kiss him again and again, and we make mad, devouring love before he, of necessity, vanishes with the full morning light. I love him too much to let him go to either heaven or hell. And when we make love, we are in heaven, a profane heaven but one of rapturous passion."

"You'se talking about burning. Do you ever think about where this is leading you when you die, where you might be goin' there would be a whole love of burning going on but the kind that really hurts forever and ever! I'm talking about hell, gal, hell, God condemns people who makes unholy love with unclean spirits. Gal, there is meant to be a separation between the living and the dead!

Ya hear me! I says this because I loves you and I fears for your precious white soul!"

"Delia, all I know is that if William were by my side in hell, it would be a heaven to me!"

"And the fire and brimstone and the worms that eat your face and flesh and brains, but you can't die, only howl in red-hot agony in hell, and the thirst, gal, the eternal thirst for a single cool drop of water or, better yet, jus a drop of Christ's all-precious blood to save you! Stop this craziness now, Amanda, before it's too late for you like it's too late for ya Aunt Eliza! She's damned too for what she does!"

Suddenly mad at Delia and her preaching and judging her, Amanda got up from Delia's bed and in an icy hauteur said to her, "I'm going to my bed now, Delia. I do not wish to be disturbed by you and your sanctimonious judging of me, Delia, not tonight, not ever, really. You leave me and William alone, Delia. He gets real mad when he's disturbed in his nights with me! You know that, don't you?"

A very hurt look came over Delia's face and she cried a little and said simply, "Yessum, I understands all right!"

"Good" was all that Amanda said as she opened the door to her own suite of rooms and closed the door a little loudly. Her parting shot to Delia was "I'm glad you understand, Delia, that way you won't get hurt!"

Then she untied her satin bathrobe, put it on the pastel pink chair near her large mirror and dresser. She sat down and combed her long, lustrous blonde hair. She wanted to look her best tonight for William. Then, after that, she lay down and knew that William would not be long in coming. She left her beside lamp on for him. "William, William, William" ran like a prayer through her fevered mind and then she did what she usually did now on such nights and waited impatiently for him!

Delia was a silly old fool about this affair of hers. Still, she did love her and was glad she had warned her not to interfere between her and William. Otherwise, Delia could be very hurt by an irate and seemingly all-powerful William. Then resting her golden head on her luxurious pillow, she waited.

An amorphous, diaphanous cloud of light began forming by her bedroom door. It swirled near her bed and then began to solidify into muscular flesh and blood. Soon, William's handsome, shaven face was smiling at her. He was dressed splendidly in his spotless Confederate gray uniform. She spread his arms wide and enfolded him.

She loved his warm, muscular embrace. Within seconds, he was naked and so was she. Every touch of his ignited a fire of passion in her that, as usual when she was with him, set to devouring her.

Suddenly delirious with passion, she was kissing him all over, even the nipples of his muscular, hairy chest. Then she tried something she hadn't ever before with him. She had, a long, long time ago, tried it with Ted, her handsome, murderous stepfather.

Now, her blood running with ecstasy in her veins, she licked the hair like a ruff under his belly button and he groaned. Then she began sucking his hard, beautiful erect penis. Unlike Ted's organ, or she assumed, all the organ of living men, William's penis did not taste sour but sweet, a little like honey.

The hardness filled her mouth totally and his hands grabbed her head up and down. Then she stopped and he suddenly entered her and ground and ground in her. She said, "Oh my god, William! I love you!" and then she climaxed with what to her was an explosion of rainbows and ecstasy.

William said, "Oh my Lord Christ," and if a ghost could climax, he did and then both collapsed into each other. Later, they made love a few more times that night. Then, before she slept in his arms, she told him of her plans to see Craig Weston in the next day or so, and he asked her why since, seemingly, he was everything to her.

She said, "I love you, William, I really do. But, William, I want to have a child and I can only have children by the living. But, don't worry, William, I'll never love Craig like I love you. If I do get pregnant, I'll have the child here and you and I can be always together anyway."

"You mean you'd have the child out of wedlock? That would hurt you socially!"

"Do you think I care? I'm now rich enough to never care about what society thinks. And, William, you could help me with the child. I'm sure he or she would be able to see and hear you and you could help me raise him."

"Oh, Amanda, my Katy who was my lover in my lifetime. She became pregnant with my baby, but she died in that condition of cholera after I'd died at Gettysburg. If you do have a baby, course I'll help you raise it. I love you no matter what, my darling!"

Then she, exhausted by her mad raptures with William, fell asleep in his arms. She really had never been happier or more in love with him for his declaration to her. Of course, he understood that if she wanted a child of her own, she needed a living lover. And best of all, he'd help her raise it. Her cup of blessings overflowed really now.

She fell asleep smiling and had dreams of herself as Katy and making love with William in the field when they had need of for their clandestine trysts. When she awoke in the morning, they only had time for some quick love-making, and then with the full morning light in the room, he disappeared, her name on his lips.

The next day, it was with decidedly mixed feelings that she called Craig Weston in the afternoon in his dorm room at Chicago University. Craig sounded very surprised, in fact, shocked, that she called him, but also happy, very happy, in fact, thrilled to hear from her.

"Like I'm so glad to hear from you, Amanda, but why, really are you calling me now?" he asked with kind of an edge in his voice.

"You and I were to meet but then you had that trouble with Judge Withers and his little KKK supporters and some people really got hurt. They all went to jail for what they tried to do to me, my visiting old Aunt Eliza, my staff and, ultimately, my mansion! They deserved to get hurt and go to jail!"

"And there were a lot of unanswered questions as to just how you, your great-aunt, and your some twelve male servants took on the KKK and won! They're pretty tough people!"

"Look, Craig, I was tougher, all right? In this life, you have to be tougher, a lot tougher than your enemies or those who mean to hurt you and yours! Don't forget, my own stepfather tried to kill me when I was fifteen after he'd killed my mother. He would have killed me, too, if I hadn't shot him before he could complete the job. I learned real early only the strong make it in life, survival of the fittest and all. Anyway, Craig," and here her own hard-edged voice changed into a lyrically happy, mellow in tone, "Look, whatever happened in the past, Craig, I still regard you warmly. How about if I take a plane tomorrow and visit you for a day or so?"

"I don't know, Amanda, I'm really busy with my studies now and all."

"Oh, Craig, when I come by tomorrow, I can tell you I won't be sleeping alone."

"Well, who will you be sleeping with then?" he asked taken a bit aback.

"In our bed together, Craig! Craig, in our bed, I'll drift off to a sound sleep after we make love at least half a dozen times! When I dated you in high school and we came so close to having sex, how I wanted to, Craig boy," she crooned into the receiver, "how I wanted to. But my dead Aunt Lavinia had made me promise to be a good girl while I was living under her roof. And when you proposed to me, how I wanted to accept, but we were a bit young, I felt. Anyway, now is different, Craig. Aunt Lavinia's will left me a fortune and I can live any way I want to now, and I will."

"Okay, he said, but if we make love, will you marry me? My parents might object, though, for your having buried your Aunt Lavinia as you did near her black Mammy. But I love you so much, Amanda, that even if they don't like this marriage, I so want to marry you, despite it all. OK?"

"Well, Craig, if they do disown you, I'll pay your way through college. The least I can do. And I think you'll be a brilliant lawyer, too. But we'll discuss marriage later. Let's see how we really click together as lovers, first, OK?"

"See you tomorrow, Amanda. Call me tomorrow morning as to when your flight is coming in. I'll be at Chicago Airport to get you. I can't wait! Just call me after 7 A.M. OK?"

"Of course, lover boy, of course, and I cannot wait to see you and I'm with you tomorrow! Until then!" And she breathed heavily and kissed heavily into the telephone receiver.

Then he thought long and hard about the upcoming visit and what it would really transpire in his life. In a way, he couldn't wait to see her but he knew there was something she wasn't telling him.

Possibly she had an ulterior motive in seeing him. Did she? He wanted to make love to her and all, but as an aspiring lawyer, he had a thirst and near-reverence for the truth which, to him, was something almost holy.

And goddamnit, there would be at least truth between him and Amanda if nothing else.

The next day, when he picked her up at the airport, to his amazement, she was dressed in black. Also, she looked even lovelier than ever. Her peaches-and-cream complexion was dazzling, her eyes even a darker shade of blue. A blue as blue as dark sapphires. Her beauty was heightened somehow in a haunting, ethereal way. And her lovely black, fashionable dress heightened, if anything, her fair beauty.

After they embraced and kissed in the airport, to the smiles of the rambling crowds milling around them.

In his car, he asked why she was dressed all in black, including black high heels on her feet.

"For my dear aunt Lavinia, of course. I made a vow to myself when she died as she did to stay in mourning attire at least a year. Anyway, take me to the most luxurious hotel in town for the weekend (it was Friday). Say we're married or whatever. Of course, darling boy, it's on me. We'll spend the whole weekend there. Then, I'll leave for my home Monday morning and you go back to school."

"Hey, if we're going to do this and say we're married at the hotel, why not get married for real soon? I want to."

In the car, Amanda kissed him suddenly, tenderly, passionately and said, "Oh, not now. Maybe not ever. I don't know. I'm all mixed up now. But on one level, I do love you. When we went steady in high school, remember all the times we made out and how I also wanted to go all the way with you, but I stopped you, sometimes, just in the nick of time! Well, that was my promise to aunt Lavinia. But now she's dead. I'm the heiress, so there is no hindrance or promise of chastity now. Anyway, I'll explain it all in more detail after we make love at the hotel. It's only fair I be at least somewhat honest with you."

"Why can't you tell me now? Tell me, is there someone else in the picture now?"

"As I just said, I'll explain everything as much as I can later. Not now. For now, let's just enjoy each other, all right?"

Sensing her mood change, Craig let it go. All he knew was that there would be a full explanation later. He'd demand it. For now, as she said, let them both just enjoy each other, and he did so want to make love to the dazzlingly beautiful girl sitting next to him in his old Buick.

Right before they got out of the Buick in from of the Vanderloo Hotel, the city's best, most luxurious hotel, she said, "Wait just a minute, Craig. It'll look more authentic if we're wearing these on our ring fingers."

And with that, she reached into her black velvet purse and took out the beautiful, somewhat ornate diamond wedding rings.

"Where did you get these?" he asked quizzically. "They're something I just couldn't afford now."

"Funny you should ask, Craig. They're my late parents' wedding rings. Actually, my late mother's and stepfather's wedding rings. The police gave them both to me after that awful scandal and tragedy happened. My aunt Lavinia kept them in her safety-deposit box. I got them after her tragic death."

"Hey, wait a minute! I positively will not wear this," and he took the man's glittering wedding ring and tossed it into her lap. "Your stepfather murdered your mother and tried to kill you. If I wear it just to convince some hotel clerk, who probably couldn't care less whether or not we really are married, I'll feel tainted and so will our love be in my eyes!"

"Oh, Craig, Craig, my honorable, sweet Craig. It's just a bit like play-acting, and the rings will help us play the part. I don't want any hint of a scandal trailing you. You are not rich yet like I am and everyone knows everyone in Richmond. Just wear it for me. Forget the kind of beastly man who wore it previously. Do it for me. They are beautiful rings and convincing. Our love, whatever love I feel for you now will cleanse and redeem those rings that came from that man, all right? Do it for me, please," she crooned, looking very beguiling indeed.

He looked at her and said, "Okay. All right. Just this once for you. But after this, promise me you will sell those rings and give the money for charity or something. I don't want your parents' evil trailing you or us. All right? Your aunt Lavinia would have fully approved over your giving the money for those rings to some worthy charity or other."

"Sure, Craig, sure, darling. Just wear the ring and play the part of my new husband. Who knows? Someday you might really be my husband. We're just going to enjoy a honeymoon, so to speak, before the wedding. Let's do it, Craig, please, Craig now."

And they wore the rings and went in and acted like a happily married young couple under an assumed name for them both, of course.

The clerk smiled at them and so did the people in the lobby at the handsome young couple. The clerk gave them the keys to what he described was a beautiful suite of rooms and did not remark that Amanda gave him cash to pay for this and not Craig. But who really cared who paid what as long as money changed hands?

The hotel bellhop took both of their light suitcases with them in the elevator and said how really it was the best suite of rooms the hotel had to offer.

Everything was light and airy and it had a beautiful view of the sky and the architectural wonders of the city of Chicago. At the door to the suite, Amanda tipped the bellhop generously and said, "Thank you, my young sir."

The boy laughed with them and said a heartfelt "Happy honeymoon, Mr. and Mrs. Van craft." The assumed name they chose. Why not, it was as rich-sounding as the ornate rings they both wore!

Craig noticed how easily and cunningly Amanda dissimulated whenever she chose and so skilled she was at it as if she herself really believed the bold-faced lies that fell from her lips. It wasn't that he didn't tell little white lies himself. Usually to spare someone's feelings, but Amanda could have been an actress they way she wove fantasy into reality or just plain colorful and elegant mendacity and bold, coy lying.

What kind of woman was this really? What the hell was he getting involved with? But the moment the door was closed on the effusive bellhop, she embraced Craig and kissed him so sweetly and passionately on his lips and she said, "Welcome to heaven, Craig, boy! Welcome to a heaven of utter bliss I don't think you'll ever forget!"

Like young lovers long before and since, they were soon naked and wrapped into each other in the large, soft couples' bed. The bedspread was ornate and shining teak and mahogany wood. The mattress firm but soft and yielding. But Amanda wasn't concentrating on the bed. This was the very first time she'd seen Craig Weston naked and he her, and both of them were very pleased with what they saw.

As he was kissing her, Amanda noted that Craig was well-built and had an athletic built. He had some reddish hair on his chest and abdomen. She began kissing not only his face but his chest and other areas.

"Oh, Amanda, here, in this college, I've dreamed of this. I so wanted to call you, but I didn't know if you'd wanted me to ever call you."

"Oh, Craig, nothing matters except the here and now between us."

Her blood began flaming in her veins and arteries. Craig was a gentle lover as if he were afraid of hurting her.

His muscular body felt very warm and good to her, and she appreciated his gentleness, too, as if she were a china, porcelain doll he was afraid of shattering. When they finally were having intercourse, she felt some ecstasy. But a little disappointed, she felt that yes, maybe Aunt Eliza was right about living men being nowhere near as intense as the dead in their amatory skills.

It didn't matter, though. She was here now to try to get pregnant, and that was all that mattered to her. Finally, she climaxed almost when Craig did. They then talked about how much this meant to them and began kissing and caressing again.

They both made love again and again. Craig enjoyed her seemingly endless passion and was frankly surprised at it. But unbeknownst to him, Amanda did have an ulterior motive. Finally, when Craig was exhausted, he just wanted to talk.

"Amanda, wouldn't you just like to be together and make love forever and ever? it could be so super, just like we had planned in high school. Our getting married and living together."

"Oh, Craig, let's not talk now about lasting commitments just yet, okay? I'm just not ready for that now. I mean, let's just give it time and see. You've yet to finish college and becoming a lawyer, just like my late stepfather was. I plan on going to college next year after I take a trip to England and Europe. I plan to take Delia with me, of course. I mean I'd love to actually see and tour in those countries whose history and literature I've studied so and loved."

"Hey, any time I talk about commitments to each other, you blow me off with your clever excuses. Tell me, I've been sensing this for a while now. There is someone else in the picture, isn't there?"

"Craig, if I told you the whole truth of it all and the situation I'm currently in you'd never believe me!"

"Why not? Give me some credit, okay? Your graet-aunt Eliza was weird enough singing that very bizarre song in what must have been her own language by her sister's coffin at your aunt Lavinia's funeral! Not that I could make heads or tails of it, but it sounded either like complete gibberish or some sort of an old witch's incantation or something."

"Well, Craig, you've heard the rumors about good old Aunt Eliza. Well, I tell you, the rumors are correct, she is a witch, a pretty damn powerful one at that! With vast power over both the living and the dead!"

"Oh, come on, Amanda! This is the twentieth century in modern-day America. I can accept that the old bat is just crazy, looney-tunes or something, but an actual witch, though she does kind of look like the old stereotype of a witch, come to think of it."

Growing more and more irritated with Craig, Amanda decided on a course of action now. She looked over the luxurious bedroom they were in. She gazed at some beautiful, crystal wine glasses by a decanter of red wine relatively near the bed.

She gazed at them and concentrated. It was all a matter of energy and will, sheer will. A witch's will!

The decanter and the glasses began shaking and tinkling and one of the five glasses moved up in the air. Craig looked shocked at Amanda and noticed her intense gaze at the levitated glass up in the air!

"Amanda," he yelled at her, "are you doing that? What is this? Are you a witch too?"

Then the floating glass uptilted in the air and soared across the room over their heads and smashed into the white wall at the other end of their bedroom!

He looked at Amanda, shocked beyond belief, and she then turned her intense blue gaze upon Craig and said to him, almost defiantly, "Yes, Craig, my boy! I am a witch with powers I am still discovering over both the living and the dead, like dear, old aunt Eliza!"

"Oh my god, this can't be real! I feel I'm trapped in some nightmare now!"

"Nightmare you said? Oh, no, Craig! You were just enjoying my charms but a short time ago. And believe me, I appreciate your love for me! I just cannot fully return it to you at this time, though I do feel something for you. But you're right, I am involved with someone else!"

"Damn you to hell, Amanda Mannon!" Craig cried to her. "Then why this, why us now?"

"Craig," she said, putting a placating hand on his shoulder, enraged as he was, "in order for you fully to understand what I'm involved in right now, I'll explain it fully to you now, but please suspend all of what you think of as what is reality and learn the world is different, far different than what you ever thought it was!"

Craig looked at her suddenly perplexed, and his shoulders fell down as if crumbled in defeat and said, "After what I just saw you did with that glass, I guess I can believe anything now. Go on, tell!"

"Craig, what I'm involved in now all began a long, long time ago. It seems there was a powerful, beautiful gypsy witch named Lily who got herself involved with a king in old England. They had a daughter whom I and all the Mannons and others descend from, and the witch powers passed along in the generations. And, Craig, I'm not just a witch but a medium too. I talk to the dead, can see them fully and interact with them, too. When I was little, I could really see them. With my mother's total neglect of me, the dead in the house were often my playmates and friends. Later I discovered the ghost of that woman named Lily and she explained it all to me. Now, Craig, I'm involved with a ghost named William. He was a Confederate officer who, like many thousands of others, was killed at Gettysburg."

Craig covered his face with his hands in horror and said, "Oh no!"

"Oh, yes, Craig. he and I are lovers and I must say he is a superb lover. He never disappoints me with his, ah, amatory skills. I've been brought to erotic heights with him I never thought possible. But as good old Aunt Eliza said, the dead are so much more intense in their appetites than the living. They have a real hunger for us, Craig, a veritable hunger for the living!"

Craig shook and looked deathly pale and said, "Don't tell me any more about it, you sick bitch! It's sort of like necrophilia. You and the ghost of a dead man. I can't imagine it!"

And he shook her hand off him and moved far from her on the bed as if he feared touching her would contaminate him.

"Well, Craig, believe it, because it's real! But you asked why I saw you and gave you my body, Craig? It was a need, a necessity, actually! Craig, whatever I feel for this William, he, being a ghost, can never sire a child with me. I needed you for that, Craig, yes, I need you for that. But you see, William understood and even said if I did get pregnant with you, he'd be around me and the baby and help me raise him nice and proper!"

"I think you are deranged, you sick, evil witch! And if there is a baby, I'll take it from you, I swear I will!"

"Really, Craig, really? You're not even a lawyer yet, though I'm sure you'll be a good one someday. And which of us is rich, and who does the law favor with a child? Usually the mother, and if the mother is rich and hires such excellent lawyers, then that seals the deal! Now, Craig, if I do have a baby with you, I'll, of course, name you as the father and give you visiting rights, and just to look a bit respectable, I might even marry you as my baby's father. But, Craig, even if we marry and live together someday, I'll never give up William. I swear his kisses drive me mad! When he and I are together it's like a primal, erotic heaven!"

Craig started laughing and crying at the same time and said, "I'll never marry you now, baby or no baby. I think you broke my heart with this obscene confession. Just leave me now, Amanda, and please don't contact me again. I don't ever want to see you again!"

Then he crumpled on the bed and started really bawling.

Amanda looked a little disgusted at him! Why was poor Craig just so sensitive, Aunt Eliza was right! Craig was a wimp!

"Oh, you fool, with what I have to give you, yes, ghosts and all, you could be so happy with me, Craig."

But he just kept on sobbing, and Amanda quickly dressed and took a cab back to the airport for a quick flight home. Home with Delia and, of course, William. She'd just wanted to be honest with Craig. If he couldn't understand and now hated her for her seeming duplicity, so be it.

If, as she hoped, she became pregnant with her short but intense encounter with Craig, she would call him and then, regardless, let the chips fall where they may.

After Amanda went back home, life continued quietly and she realized that she was in a period of waiting. Of course, William visited her nightly. In a way, she felt she was married to him for her love for him was so intense and boundless.

Lily appeared to her, too, one morning, and Amanda hadn't seen her for a while. The first thing she said to her was something she suspected already.

"You know you're pregnant, don't you? The baby's due sometime this May. May babies can be the prettiest ones I think. I think you should go to Richmond and see a doctor for a checkup and those vitamins they now give expectant mothers."

Amanda sat down at the news and said, "Wow! Lily, and Craig and I made love just three times, not even a full night. And it worked! I suppose I will write or call him with the news."

Lily frowned at her a little, "You really should consider marrying this Craig now. Just to be respectable and for the baby's sake, my dear."

"Oh, Lily, for a ghost you can be surprisingly bourgeois, you know. Craig no longer loves me, he probably hates me now after I told him about William and all."

"That was your mistake, Mandy. You should have thought he couldn't take news like that. Let me tell you he loved you all the time and, yes, even now. My advice to you is to marry him. Give your baby a respectable name and all. This baby, being yours, will have special psychic powers. It'll be a special child and will need two loving, respectable parents."

"But William said he'd be around and will help me raise him."

"Dearie, William's a ghost, or did you forget about that? When other children ask him about his father, what'll he say, his daddy's a confederate officer who appears and disappears."

Amanda began to protest and Lily said, "Dear, you may now have a lot of money but people in this region can hurt you and your child in other ways, social ways. How will your little child feel if he's not invited to any other kids' birthday parties and none of his classmates will be friends with him? Yes, William is a wonderful lover and all, but you shouldn't have told Craig about him. If Craig will still marry you, you'll have to keep your dalliances with William secret from him if you can!"

Amanda flared, "That's just it, Lily, I discovered Craig is a mild, almost boring love, he'll never bring me to the heights William can and does daily and nightly!"

"That is as may be, perhaps you can arrive with an understanding with Craig, more like an open marriage. I mean, after all, if he marries you, he'll be in a whole ultra-rich social strata now, won't he? And don't think that he doesn't know that, too! Use your wiles and beguile Craig into marrying you before your pregnancy becomes obvious and see William on the sly. Or somehow arrive at an arrangement with Craig where you do your thing and he does his. Lots of richer couples in this new society have that sort of arrangement. Now, dearie, make an appointment with a gynecologist and then, pregnancy confirmed, see a long-term obstetrician, then, everything confirmed, don't write, call Craig and see what can and should be done. Remember, once you're married, arrangements can be made between you two."

Still, Amanda hesitated in calling Craig. First she saw a Doctor Applestein. He gave her a physical and administered a pregnancy test. When the liquid in the tube went from clear to blue, he smiled at her and said that she was indeed pregnant.

Her period, which was due two weeks ago was absent, and she had begun feeling somewhat nauseous in the mornings, no vomiting, though, for which she was grateful

He gave her a rough estimate of May 10 or so for the birth. When she asked for an obstetrician he could recommend, he gave her a Doctor Michael Lewis in a different part of the city. He seemed a little taken aback that in the morning, while she felt nauseous, there had been no morning vomiting.

Still, he said, it was early in this pregnancy, and maybe she was one of the lucky women who didn't throw up in the morning. Anyway, he did prescribe some special maternity vitamins and mineral tablets which she was to take with either breakfast or lunch and that was that.

She then called Doctor Lewis, explained the situation, and made an appointment for the following week. Dr. Applestein also recommended for her maternity diet, besides lots of fresh fruit and vegetables, roast chicken, fish, and beef a few times a week for their protein and iron content. And, also, to drink several glasses of low-fat milk a day or at least lots of yogurt for the calcium and other nutrients for her coming baby.

While Amanda had never really liked milk, except chocolate milk, for her coming baby, she'd make herself drink it daily. For this new, coming baby, she'd make herself do anything, including calling Craig about her new condition.

Well, she felt she must also now tell Delia about it, too. She knew she'd need her love and care for her as much as possible. Kind, warm, loving Delia would know just how to treat her during the long months of her pregnancy. She briefly wondered how her own late mother would have reacted to her new state of being.

No, cancel that thought. Her late murdered mother would not have given two hoots about her being pregnant and would have made as cold and neglectful a grandmother as she'd been a mother to her.

At least she had Delia, she always had Delia in her life as far back as she remembered. And when she told William that night, he was ecstatic for her and swore on his honor as a Southern gentleman he would stand by her and help her take care of the coming baby.

But when she told him she might, by this pregnancy, be forced to marry Craig, he became a bit angry.

"Is it really necessary for you to do that? I can tell, you don't really love that boy. You just used him to have this baby with."

"I may love him a little or I may not. But it's his baby I now carry and this is still the good old South, William, the land of Dixie. And this child, if born illegitimate, despite my inherited wealth, would suffer scorn and rejection in this society. And despite how Craig reacted when I told him about you, about us, he might even now still love me a little. Enough, anyway, to give this coming child a name. I could give him high status and wealth and prestige in a marriage. After he and I marry, we could come to some sort of understanding where you are involved, William. For I swear, as God is my witness, William, come heaven or hell, I'll never, never give you up! Like he can have a part of me where society is concerned, and secretly, discreetly, you can have the rest."

"I already feel like killing this boy, I refuse to call him a man!" yelled William at her.

"No, William, please, no violence. I tell you he and I can arrive at a certain understanding and you won't be left out of my life or my arms at all. Okay?"

"Just trust me in this. But swear to me, no violence, please! Oh, damned it, all right, no violence! But if he ever makes you unhappy even once, I will kill the scamp! That you have my word on!"

Later, after they'd argued a bit more about it, they made love.

the next morning, she told Delia about her new condition and said she was going to call Craig about it and was sure he'd do the right thing about it and marry her.

"Honey, I jus have to ask you this, were you fool enough to tell this Craig about this William of yours?"

Amanda turned white a little and said, "Yes, Delia, I did and he reacted very badly to it. In fact, he cried like his heart was broken."

"Well, baby, that was a might foolish of you to do. I don't know iffin he will marry you now!"

"I think he will, Delia, I'm sure he will, in fact. This is his baby I carry, and don't forget, I can offer him a fortune in marriage."

Delia smiled at her and said, "Oh, at least the living now and not the dead! Have you told William to leave you alone now and clear out of this place?"

"No, I haven't and I won't, Delia! I love William totally, and I swear I'll never give him up for anything or anyone! Look, Delia, I care a lot about Craig. I needed Craig to have his baby in wedlock and all. But I will continue to see William when and where possible. Hopefully, Craig and I can arrive at some sort of understanding and have a fully open and modern marriage and all. And I want to have a real society wedding. I'll walk down the aisle all in white with a real family wedding gown and why not? Craig's family, though not exactly rich now, have been among Richmond's bluebloods for a long, long time. The wedding which, of course, I'll spend a lavish amount of money on, will make all the papers in the area. When the baby's born in May, we'll just say he came a little early!"

Delia just looked at her a little sadly and said, "This is wrong of you, so wrong, Mandy! Marriage is between a man and woman where they'll swear love to each other and no other for life, come sickness and health and that's it, I says! With your looks and your riches now you might get Craig to marry you for this baby's sake, but if you's still want William too, it'll never last! He'll divorce you! No man of any honor will put up with a cheating wife, money or no money, especially if the lover is not even a living man but a goddamn spook, a ghost from the old Civil War! Yes, he might still marry you, but please, please, I begs you to start the marriage honorably on your part, sugar, please!"

Amanda flared at her, "Look, Delia, lots of people who are wealthy have understandings in their marriages whereby, as long as a public spectacle doesn't ensue, they each see other people. This is modern life, after all, I'm sure Craig and I can arrive at some sort of understanding."

"You is supposing wrong, Mandy. You see William for your pleasures and he'll divorce and leave you! Oh, your baby will have a name and all, but you'll be left with raising it with only William to help."

Amanda suddenly looked deeply at Delia and said, "If we get divorced, we get divorced, Delia. But you'll still help me raise the baby."

"A course, I will, Mandy acourse I will! Poor little baby is going to be raised fatherless with just a ghost for a daddy! Acourse I'll be here for you and this baby. But I begs you, if Craig does propose marriage now, start out fresh and honorable and all and have no other but him!"

"Oh, Delia, I know you mean well and love me, but I just can't give William up, not now, not ever! And don't even continue to ask it of me, please!"

Delia just looked at Amanda sadly and disappointedly but, in the end, promised she'd stay and help her with the coming baby.

She called Craig at his college the next day in the afternoon. He recognized her mellifluous voice immediately and sounded a bit surprised and a little glad, actually, to be hearing from her after a few months of silence.

After packing in questions about his health and how were his studies going, she, as calmly as possible, gave him the news about her present condition. There was a pause, even a shocked silence coming from his end of the receiver.

Then he asked suddenly, "Are you sure this baby's mine, Amanda?"

"What do you mean, Craig? You are the only living man I've been with since I visited you a couple of months ago. Who else's baby could this baby?"

"Oh, I don't know, Amanda. From our last conversation, you sounded randy and crazy enough to try anyone or anything! Listen to me, if we do marry for this baby's sake, you must give up this William!"

"Oh, Craig, do you know what I could offer you in this marriage? Riches you could only imagine. You wouldn't need your narrow-minded parents' approbation or money to finish your schooling and become a professional lawyer. I'd do that for you! And if you married me in what I plan, a big Richmond society wedding, it would elevate you to the Richmond's upper strata almost immediately. Remember, it was a state your people were once in but lost in the depression. Whatever your parents tell you they may think of me, believe me, they will appreciate the money and status being connected to me will give you and them. Let's be real here, all right?"

"Real politic, hey, Mandy? But if I marry you, I expect you to love and be faithful only to me!"

"And I will be to you, with the living, Craig! But the other thing, William, I'll see as discreetly as possible. Many upper-class couples have an 'understanding about such things, Craig. You know it. I know it. And it's not like I'd be cheating on you with a living man, only William!"

"Amanda, I don't ever know if I can share you with even a ghost! All right? What you are doing is abnormal. Look at that crazy great-aunt of yours, Eliza. Is that how you want to wind up?"

"Oh, Craig, marry me, all right! Fly in to see me tomorrow and we can work put what needs to be worked out like any modern couple who will be the absolute cream of Richmond society! Our wedding will be the social event of the year in Richmond! At least I'll plan it that way. Through me, your family could reconnect to the power and prestige they had enjoyed in Richmond society. Think of that. Just come here and marry me and we'll work things out. I do long to see you, Craig, and make love with you. I promise you a honeymoon you'll never forget!"

After some minutes of silence on his part, he said, "If you are pregnant with my child, I guess I'll have to do something."

"Right, Craig, our wedding will be in all the society pages in this city. I'll make sure we'll make the social register, and when our baby's born, he'll definitely be in the social register!"

"Since when did you really care so much about Richmond high society, Mandy? You never seemed to before!"

"Now, Craig, my being pregnant has made me reconsider a lot of things!"

"All right, Mandy. I'll take the first flight in tomorrow."

"Good, honey, and when the baby comes in May, I'll just tell everyone, he was a bit premature. I'll give the lie that the baby was a honeymoon baby!"

"As I discovered from the last time you were here in the hotel with me, you can lie pretty adroitly, Amanda."

"It's up there with the skills I honed with being a survivor, baby. Just come and we'll work it all out. I love you, darling!"

With that, the call ended. Good! Craig had capitulated and she and he could marry and hopefully work some sort of marital arrangement out.

That coming week, she'd work out all the details for the coming wedding. It would be a lot of work on her part, but she knew she'd love each minute of it!

One month later, October 1968

It was indeed the wedding of the century in Richmond, Virginia. For weeks, the papers had written of nothing else but the coming wedding of the city' debutante heiress-socialite, Amanda Mannon marrying a handsome and brilliant law student, Craig Weston of an equally blue-blooded family if not as currently affluent as his bride's.

The biggest and most historic St. Paul's Cathedral Episcopal Church was the church chosen. The reception was going to be held afterwards at the Hyatt-Regency Hotel and was to be totally lavish.

While not being very popular in Richmond for her outspokenly liberal views and unusual family background, when Amanda had called the papers and told them of her engagement to Craig Weston, the papers ate it up.

The Westons had once been the grandest and wealthiest of families in Richmond. While that day had passed, their name alone commanded a lot of acclaim and respect.

And with the engagement of Craig Weston to his wealthy debutante heiress, whatever her eccentricities, this was an occasion to be celebrated.

Going through her late and much missed Aunt Lavinia Mannon's list of society friends and distant relatives, Amanda had gilded wedding invitations sent to some girlfriends from high school and to all of the prominent families in Richmond and thereabouts.

The receivers of such florid wedding invitations accepted with alacrity and by marrying into a revered family like the Westons, the more questionable reputation of Amanda Mannon and Eliza was effectively forgotten and glossed over to celebrate such a happy event as this coming wedding.

And Craig and Amanda were both such a stunningly beautiful young couple. Well, wearing the most beautiful tulle and satin and lace white embroidered gown that had cost a great deal to create, carrying a lush bouquet of pink, red, and white roses in her hands, Amanda looked like a ravishing dream.

She was being walked down the aisle, having no male family member but by her lawyer who'd read out her late aunt's will effectively making her an heiress. Amanda, though somewhat in love with Craig, had chosen the lawyer as the father figure at her wedding to remind Craig and his parents that while the lineage of the Westons may have been impeccable, that she indeed was the one with the money.

In fact, she was paying for this whole white wedding and reception and the two-week honeymoon in Paris. When Craig, dressed in a dashing tux joined her at the altar, he looked so handsome. Maybe, just maybe, she could come to love Craig completely and free herself from William's spell over her, then she could live a normal life with Craig, a normal life, period.

Then, as the Episcopal bishop was speaking holy words over the young couple and people were crying with joy in the pews, Amanda saw a figure materialize right near her on her right-hand side. Oh god, as if summoned by her newly treasonous thoughts about him, it was William as dashing and handsome as ever in his impeccable gray Confederate uniform with the gold braids and the medals. He looked at her so longingly and she melted inside for him. They had made love last week when Craig was away, back at school to finish a semester. But this wasn't fair at all! She had told him to stay away from this, her wedding to Craig Weston!

But god, William was so beautiful, his uniform showed to good effect his rippling muscles that she remembered so well.

Craig looked at her seemingly blank-faced staring at nothing on her right side and nudged her and she came to just in time to hear the bishop ask her her wedding vows. She was fine with that until she said, "I vow to take Willi, oh, I mean Craig for better or worse in sickness and health as long as we both do live."

The bishop looked at her questioningly and Craig looked angrily at her. Fortunately most of the people in the pews hadn't caught the little faux pas, and Amanda hurriedly ran on with her vows which now she had no intention of keeping to Craig, for she knew in her heart she loved William overwhelmingly.

William had dissolved into nothing, and none of the people there had seen his ghostly form. But Craig knew that this ghost William had put in an appearance and had confused Amanda with the names at this most inappropriate time in their wedding. But he knew that she still loved William. But Amanda was so beautiful. He'd work so hard, very hard to win her love.

He had one advantage in that. He was a living man who could make really passionate love to Amanda. And it was his baby she carried, though, as far as he knew, no one in the church or the city knew of her condition.

Time for that later on. The wedding reception was wonderful and would be the talk of the town for many years to come. There were six courses of French cuisine with its rich, creamy dishes. Amanda's chief chef Marcel had supervised the cooking staff of the Hyatt-Regency for the feast.

There were many toasts to the wedding couple, too. Everyone was in a very jovial mood. No one seemed to mind that Delia was seated near the wedding couple and looked ecstatic to see her

Amanda properly wedded and all. Craig himself liked Delia very much, recognizing as he did Delia's genuine love for Amanda.

He also believed the fact that from Amanda's infancy on, if Delia hadn't been there, caring, loving, and nurturing Amanda while Aurelia, her mother had done her own hedonistic nympho life, Amanda probably wouldn't have survived her infancy or early childhood.

Besides that, it had been nearly two decades since integration had been forced in the South. And while the new lifestyle didn't suit everybody, most people were getting adjusted to it. There were fewer and fewer KKK cross burnings.

Of course, a lot of the racial hatred and bigotry had gone beneath most people's collective psyche to a large degree. At any rate, most people who were acquainted with the Mannons knew the maid-servant Delia was a fine Christian black woman who loved Amanda like her own daughter or granddaughter and would die for her if necessary.

Even the most conservative members of the old south could accept that fact and the fact that Delia had been instrumental to Amanda's very survival in her neglected and horrible childhood and adolescence.

Plus the fact that old Aunt Lavinia had adopted Amanda and had made her her heir had put the people of Richmond in a more accepting, forgiving mood. Lavinia had been a Catholic paragon of charity and virtue for many years in the elevated and rarified society of Richmond. They forgot quickly about the bizarre antics of Aunt Eliza and all her craziness.

The wedding augured well for the future as far as the people of Richmond were concerned. After the wedding reception, which was written of in all the city's papers for several days afterward, the wedding couple was driven to the bride's mansion, the former home of her aunt Lavinia.

Everything looked spotless. The servant staff, out of their love and loyalty to Lavinia and now Amanda, had been most assiduous in their cleaning and decorating the place for the newly married couple.

Bouquets of flowers were everywhere, adding sweet fragrances to the air as well as their pastel beauty to the eye.

Amanda's suite of rooms now had a little chandelier in the bedroom which cast glittering prismatic lights over the room. As did the several other larger chandeliers in the downstairs areas. The whole establishment looked both dazzling and lovely.

The maids Rita and Margaret and even Delia assisted in undressing and redressing Amanda for her wedding night with Craig into a lovely Parisian-style silk pink and white nightgown. Delia even insisted on combing Amanda's long golden hair out for her.

Then, at a cue, Delia kissed her goodnight and left, and Amanda found herself in her big bridal bed, awaiting Craig. The door opened and Craig came out, swiftly removing his red silk bathrobe. Studying him a moment, Amanda noticed, as if for the first time, how handsome Craig really was. And he was nicely, athletically built, too. And best of all, his amazing amatory abilities had been building in both skill and sheer passionate fire.

Each time, they'd secretly made love in the weeks before the wedding he had brought her to greater and greater heights of ecstasy and she him. It was hard to tell which turned her on more: Craig's handsome face, his kind, blue-green eyes, or his somewhat strong, rugged built. She also loved the fact his chest was strong-looking and covered slightly with some brown-red hair. She wondered momentarily if their coming baby in May would have Craig's brown-red hair or her golden color.

As a momentary thought, her murdered mother had had her colored hair, too then she forgot about her dead mother entirely as Craig silently began passionately kissing her. She began kissing him back, his now practiced touch and muscled body gaining over her, igniting passionate fire from deep within her.

She began kissing his not only handsome face but, going further, his strongly-muscled neck and, her head going down further, his muscular chest and began lapping the hair on his belly and, further down, perfecting a skill she now was very good at, began sucking his oh-so-delicious and strong, fully erect penis.

She had heard from some old girlfriends from that the art of fellatio was just that, an art to be assiduously learned and then enjoyed. She had heard from said girlfriends that they did it to please and titillate their boyfriends, more as a duty than an enjoyment. But contrary to that, Amanda really enjoyed, indeed, relished such an art, and she'd had no complaints on that score from her long-dead, murderous stepfather, the ghost William, or Craig!

Those men positively were ecstatic about her skills in that department. She'd read somewhere in a slightly profane history book that Catherine the Great of Russia was also highly skilled in that department on her many amours.

Craig was moaning heavily above her while Amanda was enjoying him; she just imagined that it was William above her she was avidly sucking and fucking. Oh, yes, when she'd seen William in all his uniformed masculine beauty at her wedding, she'd melted inside. Oh, why, she nearly thought, had she married Craig Weston anyway?

True, she did feel some love for Craig and her coming baby needed a name and a father. But her fate was so cruel. Why couldn't it have been William all along? The very thought of him set her on fire. When Craig now entered her, it was her turn to begin groaning and when Craig finally climaxed, so did she and almost simultaneously, she began groaning, "Yes, oh, yes, William, do it to me again. Oh, William, you are my god!"

A suddenly furious Craig began roughly shaking her on the bed.

"Amanda, amanda," he suddenly screamed at her, livid with rage now. "Hey, you married me, yet at the wedding ceremony, you said William not my name at the sealing of vows! And I know you somehow saw this ghost, William! He's a fucking ghost, damnit, a fucking civil war ghost, over a hundred years old! You married me, damnit, you married me and it's my baby you're carrying! Doesn't that mean anything to you at all?"

Amanda angrily shook his near-throttling hands off her and screamed at him, "Hey, you rather willingly married me, knowing William was still in the picture. I married you hoping we could work something out because as God is my witness come heaven or hell, I cannot give up William. Every time I even glance at him, I melt with desire!"

Craig only looked at her and punched his pillow and said, "Damnit all, how can I win over a fucking ghost? This is all insane, just insane!"

"Craig, believe me, I do care about you, I do, I do. And I swear I will be faithful to you with the living, period, but don't ask me to give up William, because I cannot! He is as essential to me as the air I breathe, I cannot and will not give him up! Maybe it would help you if you took your pleasures with another woman, and we both could have an open mariage like some couples do!"

Craig just groaned and turned away to the wall and willed himself to sleep from what was to him a horrible and untenable situation. His last thoughts before he slipped into unconsciousness were should he start divorce proceedings tomorrow?

But damnit, this was Amanda and he did love her, what was he to do?

Amanda drifted off to sleep gradually. She knew this was a bad and rocky start to her marriage, but she did love William and that was that. She fell quickly to sleep and found herself walking in that now familiar pasture where she was wearing that period-piece blue dress and she knew her name was Katey.

Then the handsome William was there before her and she felt like swooning in his arms and he covered her face with kisses and they tumbled to the ground, and instantly, they were both soon naked and she was kissing him all over and he her.

But then she woke up. She sensed William near her bed. She saw Craig was lying, his face still to the wall. She looked around her room and said, "William, William, I know you're there! Please reveal yourself to me!"

Then, out of some shimmering diaphanous light, William suddenly materialized by her bed. God, he was so stunningly handsome and so well-built. He put her new husband Craig to shame by a country mile, really. He began walking toward her, and she flung her arms wide open for him and soon, almost instantly, she was naked too.

The rapture which soon totally engulfed her was a higher and greater degree than any she had hitherto experienced before with him. It was as if her were trying to prove to her that, not just his love-making but his very love itself were superior, vastly superior to anything Craig or any mere mortal man could possibly give her. Soon, too soon, really she was gasping and breathing hard in her multiple orgasms. Craig soon woke up with the noise and heard rumbling and glanced around and was startled out of his wits to see the dark-haired man on top of Amanda who was looking at him startled herself but with a surprised and ingenuous look on her face.

But instantly Craig's shock and fear turned into an all-consuming rage at both Amanda and this fuckng ghost, William. He struck Amanda in the face hard, and she cried out in pain, covered her face and moved away from both William and Craig in the bed.

Then Craig began pummeling and hitting William as hard as he could, ghost or no ghost. William seemed totally unaffected by Craig's blows and looked at Craig with eyes blazing blue with hatred and fury. He didn't punch or pummel Craig but simply grasped two very strong hands around Craig's neck and began really squeezing, and Craig couldn't grasp the ghostly hands from around his neck.

He began violently choking and turning blue and looked at a blank-faced Amanda with his eyes suddenly imploring her. Amanda just stared for precious seconds to herself, and as if suddenly coming to herself out of some mental fog, she screamed at William to stop, stop choking Craig, to please don't kill him for her sake.

William suddenly looking shocked and surprised at Amanda, grunted, and released his hands from Craig's neck and throat with a disgusted look at Craig.

He said in a loud, stentorian voice to Craig, "You ever hit my Amanda again or even make her unhappy and I will kill you and nothing you or anyone can do will stop me! Do you understand, little man?"

Craig looked at William fearfully and nodded yes, he did understand completely. Smiling at Amanda, William suddenly disappeared.

Rubbing his hands around his bruised neck and throat, Craig said slowly to Amanda, "Hey, why did you wait so long before you said something to your ghost-lover. The bastard almost killed me!"

"Why didn't I interfere right away, Craig? To teach you a lesson, Craig! And I swear you ever hit me again or even, as William said, make me unhappy, I will call William and watch, gloating, while he does kill you! Understand, Craig, baby! I will not take that shit from any man, ever! My stepfather killed my mother and tried to kill me but I killed him myself first! Life is for the strong, Craig! I thought, maybe, we could work something at something together with William, but I guess not, Craig!"

"You guessed right, Amanda! You didn't even get beyond the honeymoon before you were cheating on me with this William right in front of me! No man can accept that!"

"Really, Craig? Listen, if you'd been a little more, ah, friendly and accommodating to William, he might have let you join us together in what the French blithely call a ménage-a-trois. Such things are not unheard of among some married couples."

"Well, not this one, Amanda. And that you could think of such a thing proves you are a really sick, depraved woman. I guess the apple doesn't fall too far from the tree, does it, Amanda, hey!"

Knowing he was referring to her dead, nympho mother Aurelia, Amanda got really furious and said, "You get out of here now, Craig, you little bourgeois choir-boy! Go back to your parents like good little boys do! Pack up and get out of this house now!"

"Oh, don't worry, I will, Amanda, I will!"

"Anyway, I have what I wanted from you, Craig, my baby will have a name, yours, anyway! And I may or may not give you visiting rights! But just leave now, Craig, before I do let William kill you!"

Craig scrambled from the honeymoon bed, dressed, went downstairs, packed a hurried suitcase, and called a cab to leave.

Before he left Amanda's bedroom, he said to her, "I'm leaving you and William together, Amanda! I never want to see you again! And your poor aunt Lavinia must be spinning in her grave!"

"Get out, get out!" And Amanda grabbed an unopen bottle of pink champagne at his retreating form, and it smashed on the door just as Craig left the room.

He felt so relieved to be leaving this deranged, ghost-infested mad house and this madwoman with her unnatural lusts. He really never wanted to see Amanda Mannon ever again. As for their coming child, he'd cross that bridge when he came to it.

The next morning, Delia knocked on Amanda's bedroom door at a relatively late morning hour for the consideration of the newly wedded couple.

Amanda inside said, "Come in, Delia, please help me with cleaning up and dressing for breakfast."

Startled to hear only Amanda and not Craig Weston at all, Delia bared her fat form into the room and found only Amanda in her wedding bed alone and with a nasty-looking bruise on the left side of her face.

She ran to her and screamed in shock and fright, "What happened to you? Did Craig hit you?"

"Yes, he did, Delia. Anyway soon, I'll be filing for a quick divorce from him for emotional and physical abuse. I'll see my lawyer today and have pictures taken of my bruised face as evidence. Craig Weston will not get a single penny from me or my estate."

Delia slumped down, sitting on Amanda's side of the bed and knowing there was a lot more to it than Amanda was telling her.

"Tell me now, why did you and Craig have such a terrible fight in which he used violence? Was the ghost William involved? Is that it?"

Amanda looked at Delia and smiled cynically at her.

"I guess I could never hide anything from you, Delia, could I?"

"Well, William showed up even when I'd told him not to appear at my wedding and honeymoon. But he did, Delia, and of course, one thing led to another and we made love and Craig woke up and caught us in flagrante delicto as it were and hit me hard and began hitting William. William started strangling Craig and then I begged him to stop. But I was still furious with Craig for having so hit me. After William vanished, Craig and I had words and I told him to leave, which he did and now I am alone. But I do have William, thank god! nd I got what I wanted from Craig, my coming baby will at least have a name."

"Oh, Amanda, this was so, so foolish of you to see William and make love wid this ghost on your own honeymoon wid Craig. Now what will you do?"

"As I said, my baby will have Craig's name. William has sworn he will help me raise it."

Delia said, appalled at Amanda, "Look, William's a ghost! How much care can he give this coming child?"

"Look, William is very physical for a ghost! If he said he'd help, he will and whatever will be will be, Delia." Grasping Delia's hand, she said, "You'll be here with me too, Delia, to help me raise the baby when it's born! Plus, there's the ghost Lily, though I don't see her too often, but she does love me or seem to and has always given me the truth in my problems."

Delia looked at Amanda very angrily and took her hands and pounded them on the bed's silken covered mattress emitting an angry, frustrated groan of unnph!As her hands pounded on the mattress as if she wanted desperately to finally pound some sense into Amanda's beautiful blonde head!

She hissed at her, "Lor, girl, I raised you. I love you but you's acting like you ain't got a lick of sense! Your coming baby may not be bastard born now and have a name, but your new husband is a really good man and would be a great father to him. You turn to spirits when what you need is simple human help and love from the living in the real world! The dead can't help you much in the affairs of the living, especially where raising a lil child is concerned. Call Craig back I say! He's your husband now, and if he did hit you, you gave him real good reason to by making your sick love with a ghost on your own honeymoon! Please," a pleading tone in Delia's voice, "call Craig back and send William very far away permanently! Please!"

Amanda shook her head violently from side to side and shrieked at Delia, "After this shiner on my face, never! No man treats me like day-old garbage and hits me and demeans me to my face! At least William wouldn't do that! He really does love me, Delia, and as I've said, when we make love, tit's heavenly. Well, Delia," she said, putting a hand on Delia's shoulder, "leave me now, please. I know what you think. I have to call my lawyer and have him come here to take a picture of my bruised and battered face. They say one picture is worth a thousand words!"

Delia got up, still imploring Amanda not to do that but to call Craig ack, as if he would now.

Silly Delia did not understand at all! She couldn't have Craig back. If he got mad at her and struck her again, William really would kill him and she'd have a body to explain to the police and the authorities!

No, she'd divorce Craig as expeditiously as possible. She picked up the phone and called her lawyer's home number, it being a Sunday and his office perforce being closed. all she thought while she dialed her lawyer and explained the total disaster her beginning honeymoon had become, was that things would work out for her and her coming baby.

After all, she had William always and she had Lily. Things may be a bit bizarre to most regular, normal people, but with proof of Craig's potential for violence to her, all she wanted was William, period.

In the afternoon, her lawyer, a debonair Jack Dearborne came with a flash instamatic camera as requested. He got all the particulars of Amanda's sad story. Well, she didn't tell him a word about William and William's involvement in triggering Craig's jealous rage which had caused him to hit her and demean her.

All she said was that Craig was irrationally, uncontrollably jealous, and they'd argued and fought about it and he had violently hit her. She wanted a divorce for physical and emotional abuse as quickly as possible.

After the lawyer took the pictures of her bruised and battered face, during which the white flash of the camera blinded her a little while. Mr. Dearborne asked if she wanted to press criminal charges on Craig for his violent assault. She said no and smiled and said she just wanted this divorce as quickly and as quietly as possible. And as discreetly as possible, too.

Only if Craig said false, horrible things about her in court would she press charges for assault and battery. But she had a feeling, he would make such false, sensationalist claims about her in court.

As to property and money, she didn't want to give this Craig Weston a dime. Let him pay for his own lawyer in this divorce. With the evidence of his brutality to her now evident, she could make his and his family's name mud in this city.

The lawyer told her that in this, with the pictures of her, she had Craig at a distinct disadvantage and probably Craig also wanted to be swiftly divorced from her now.

She did tell the lawyer that she was now pregnant. That had been the principal reason for marrying Craig to begin with. Now, at least, her coming baby would be legitimate and have Craig's surname.

"Are you thinking of future child support from this Craig?"

"Are you kidding? Craig won't be a practicing lawyer for two years yet. And maybe I'll give him visiting rights and maybe I won't."

"Now, Amanda Mannon, don't let your marital rage blind you about this. Craig seemed like such a good, decent boy. Obviously, he is not now. But every child needs a father as well as a mother."

Amanda smiled a bit and laughed a little and said, "Even if I never see Craig again, ever, my child will have good male support and upbringing without Craig. Trust me!"

"Well," the lawyer said unctiously, "do as you think best. I'll call Craig Weston Monday morning with this news and the pictures and, hopefully, he won't fight about a quick divorce."

"Good day, Amanda."

"Good day, Mr. Jack Dearborne, I'm sure I can trust you in this matter. Just call me after you see Craig, and we'll proceed, hopefully, with this matter as quietly and discreetly as possible. Because of my dear, departed aunt Lavinia, whom I loved very much and was really a holy woman, I do want this resolved as discreetly as possible with no mention in the papers at all. Got me? No publicity of this matter, please."

"Well, Amanda, we will try, but you did have a very public wedding and all. In fact, just a day ago, it was a cause celebre in this city, and well, even if it's kept out of the papers, word will inevitably get out in this city and people will wonder and talk."

"Let them! I just want as little publicity in this city as possible. Now, I pay you a monthly retainer, a high one, as you are one of the best lawyers in this damn city. Please follow my wishes as much as possible."

"Yes, Amanda," he bowed, took her hand, and kissed it and left the house as quietly as he'd entered it, and that was that on the matter and Amanda tried to dismiss the unpleasant situation as much as possible. She had William to look forward to.

She called Rita the maid in charge of the domestic staff and told her to tell the rest of the staff to not bother her that day and to decline any visitors who came by chance to the house. To tell all and sundry that she was a bit ill and wished not to be disturbed that day.

Rita, wondering where this new groom Craig was and if the large, purple bruise on Amanda's face was his doing, as was probable she thought. After all, this new bridegroom was, for all intents and purposes, nowhere to be found in the huge mansion. Already there'd been some talk among the staff which Delia, Amanda's personal maid, had heard of the talk and had been vexed at the talk and had told the staff to be quiet about the matter.

Well, inside the mansion, they would be quiet about it if they valued their positions of course, they'd be discreet. But outside of the mansion, what they said outside was their affair. As she wandered down the hall from Amanda's new bridal suite, Rita thought it was really too bad that the bridal couple had broken up right on the honeymoon. And they were both supposed to go to Paris for their honeymoon. And Amanda had seemed so happy about this Craig and her coming marriage to him.

Well, it apparently came to naught. Too bad, but it was entirely Amanda's business, and if this Craig had hit her face so violently, she was better off without him indeed.

But she'd also heard through the staff grapevine that Amanda was pregnant now. Well, with the wedding, at least the coming child would be legitimate, if only barely.

Anyway, Amanda was now very rich, and as well Rita knew, the rich were different and didn't abide by the same morals and mores the more common people did in society. But it was a pity both about the physical trauma and the early breakup of what had been a very dazzling wedding. A pity, yes, but really none of her business.

In the meantime, Amanda went to her door and locked it. Not that with her orders to Rita there was any need to, but she definitely wanted to now maintain her absolute privacy in the house for the rest of the day and night. She'd later call Rita downstairs with the staff number and have her or some other maid bring up her lunch and later dinner, knock on the door, and leave the tray on the floor outside the door.

There she could be absolutely alone with William now. There had been great stress and tension about the whole breakup with Craig and then Delia's remonstrances about it to her. Only her wonderful lover William could be the soothing balm for her agitated nerves. Oh, he could make love so deliciously, so beautifully.

Good, she lay back on her bed, drank some still chill purple grape juice. After the wedding, there could be no more booze in her diet. She did, after all, now have the baby sleeping and developing in her womb.

She'd take her prescribed prenatal vitamin-mineral pills with lunch. And later on in the pregnancy, the ghost Lily had said that raspberry tea was very good for prepping her womb and uterus for the coming birth. With the way she now felt about Craig, though he was a handsome man, she hoped her baby didn't look too much like him.

She liked the fact that with those pictures of her battered and bruised face, taken that very morning by her savvy lawyer, she probably would be quite from to forbid Craig from ever adding the baby or having anything to do with the child or her also.

Craig was such a fool. By physically attacking her, he had fallen right into a trap she so readily thought of when he'd hit her. Deny him any visiting rights with his child and any future contact with her. No man dared to treat her so vilely. That Craig had been unduly provoked by catching her in the bed they shared as newlyweds, with William was his stupid mistake he'd pay now dearly for.

She'd gone into this marriage just to give her baby a name and that was all. With the marriage license she now had that and she had gotten with Craig what she wanted from him, a coming, she hoped, healthy baby and a legitimate name for this child.

That was now all, and that was all she now wanted. Craig was a brutal fool, and she did not suffer fools gladly. Let him be some ambulance-chasing lawyer or something. She didn't care what he became. Just stay out of her heart and the baby's life, please. And the divorce should take care of that nicely.

True, she had used him for her own ends, but so what? In this world, people used each other every day. And Craig had used her by readily agreeing to this marriage in the first place. In fact, he knew also in the first place that while she liked him well enough, he knew because she had told him before that his suspicions about her were only too correct. She was really in love with her ghost-lover, William, and wasn't about to give him up, ever.

She knew, in fact, at least in part he'd married her for her inherited wealth and the social prominence that went with it. In fact, he'd been quite beguiled, not just with her beauty but her great wealth. And so had his parents, for that matter. Far from banning their son from marrying her, just a while ago, his mother had slapped Craig in public away from her at Aunt Lavinia's burial. After she'd inherited her said aunt's fortune, they were much more accepting of her.

And really, she thought, in this world, money talked and that was all that mattered apparently. With the upbringing she'd had with such a depraved, deplorable mother and quasi-incestuous, murderous stepfather, she had few illusions about anything or anyone.

She had come to really love her aunt Lavinia who'd loved her and meant only to do good by her. But as she'd discovered, even Aunt Lavinia had had her own past and secrets to conceal.

As she lay on the bed and listened to some very relaxing music from one of the classical music stations on her radio, she suddenly saw a white glimmer in the corner of her bedroom. Aha, she felt William, her lover, William, in the room. She knew it was William in her heart.

The glimmering light swiftly materialized into William's darkly handsome face and semi-solid form. And he was naked for her and visibly aroused. Oh, it would be a most delicious time with him, she needed him now so much, so badly!

On her bed, she opened up her arms to him. Oh god, he was so beautiful! He swiftly glided across the floor by her side on the bed. She took her hand and caressed his strong, sturdy chest, running her hands into his hairy chest with one hand and grabbing and rubbing his erect penis.

He groaned a little and lay on top of her. Her bedclothes were off in a moment, and he began sucking her large pink and white breasts and she began to moan to herself. She felt herself go wet with lush desire in her most innermost parts.

William got on top of her, and kissing her wildly on her face and her body all over and entered her and she felt mad paroxysms of pleasure in wave after wave of ecstasy all through her. She saw rainbows of pastel colors like tingling novas in her mind. She kissed him and sucked him all over and then William pounded and pounded inside her, and finally William groaned in some orgasmic release and herself experienced wave after wave of physical rapture in her climax with William.

Then she thought of something odd and said to him, "William, it's broad daylight now, but you're not disappearing on me, what happened?"

"It's your desire for me which has daily grown stronger and stronger for me which has given me the strength to stay a long while now in the daylinht instead of fading away in the night and early morning. I can now stay with you for many hours of the day and night, too, if that is your wish."

"My wish, my wish, William! It is my innermost mad desire for you to have you with me day and night always, William, always! Oh, William, you know I'm divorcing Craig quickly I hope. Thanks to you I'm sure he won't contest it! He was a fool for striking me so hard he left visible bruises on my face. The pictures my lawyer took should damn him in court! And he won't get one thin dime from me, nothing, in fact! But I have from him all I want from him, a coming baby and now a legitimate name for this baby! It's all I want, and because of those pictures, William, I'm sure I can deny him visiting privileges with the child when it comes and I will! My baby will have you to act as its father! Yes, I think I'll like that arrangement much better. I'm pretty sure my baby will be able to see you, too, and interact with you and other ghosts, too. Lily the ghost says it is hereditary in my family! And we can be one happy family, William," He kissed her again heatedly and said, "If this man, Craig, ever seeks you out again, Amanda, I'll kill him with my bare hands, I swear I will! Still, though, your time here and now is very different from mine when I was alive. In my time on earth, if a man struck his wife in anger or even whipped her in discipline, nothing was ever made of it. It was considered his own business and divorce was not an option for the woman. One sometimes, heard of women poisoning their beating husbands, but if they were ever caught doing that, the women were hanged as a matter of course. Of course, if I'd ever had the chance to marry my love, Katy, and you are her reborn, I would never have struck her. But we both died before we could ever marry! But I have you now and you have me and now the coming baby, Katy my love."

"William, William," Amanda said, "this talk of reborn lives makes me so anxious, so hungry for the here and now, William, please, please let's make love again, please, again! I think I was born insatiable for you and only you!"

Later that day, William disappeared and said he'd be back later that night for her, but for now she needed a rest, anyway. She mustn't strain her vital parts for the coming baby too much. It might be dangerous, and he wanted her to rest more and more as the pregnancy progressed.

And so, William having left her, she relaxed and napped, then awakening with a maid knocking at the locked door with her lunch. Aha, it was one of Marcel's best creations, some creamy fish dish with spinach and corn and radishes. Lately, she had been giving the chefs downstairs to include plenty of fruits and vegetables in her meals of fish, chicken, and occasional red meat.

It was delicious, of course, as were all of Marcel's creations, but now the cooked vegetables in the meals would help ensure a healthy baby. Almost absently, as directed by her obstetrician, she took her prescribed vitamins and minerals right after she finished her lunch. And for dessert, she had, as requested some strawberry Jell-O and a banana and a red, delicious apple instead of some creamy French pastry. She didn't want to get too fat with this pregnancy, though she knew some weight gain was inevitable, even, of course, healthy!

After she gave birth, though, she wanted to regain her normal figure as soon as possible. That afternoon, she rested, read one of her favorites, Emily Bronte's *Wuthering Heights*. Oh, the mad passion of Catherine Earnshaw and Heathcliffe, transcending death itself, reminded her of her own mad passion with William that really had transcended death and time itself.

She also loved reading the descriptions of the stark English moorlands in England. After the baby was born and old enough, she felt she'd visit England herself, and bring Delia along, too, and also take in a good deal of Western Europe, too. She'd heard England itself was one of the most haunted countries in the world. Well, it had the history to prove it!

The Tower of London, supposedly, was very haunted. But considering its history, why not? When she'd read of the sad fate of the two little princes in the tower, she'd actually cried a little. How awful! Her baby now, though, would be loved by her and William and protected like no other child on earth.

When she was a young girl, she'd promised herself if she ever had a baby, unlike her horrible, totally neglectful mother, her baby would be loved and protected completely by her.

When she woke up from her nap, she called downstairs for Delia, and after giving her a warm kiss which Delia was a little surprised at and said she was sorry she had had some stern words with her earlier. But she had to understand, she no longer loved Craig Weston and was dissolving the marriage, in fact. All she cared about was the legitimacy of her coming baby by Craig. And of course, there was the indelicate matter of William.

She said to Delia that while she knew it went against her beliefs about the boundaries of the living and the dead, she loved William completely and would never give him up, period, so please, please, do not reprove her about it.

She knew that she, Amanda, had been born with the gift of seeing and interacting with the so-called dead. She had taken that occult talent one step further, and as God was her witness, William was the best lover anywhere possible and she was very happy with him as she'd never been happy with Craig or any other living man.

Please give her the courtesy she would give any other adult woman and not be judgmental of her private life with William as it was entirely her own business and no one else's.

Delia had cried a little and said that as she loved her as her own daughter or granddaughter she couldn't help but be concerned about what she viewed as an unhealthy, even unnatural relationship, but she would keep her opinions to herself from now on. It was just too bad she was losing Craig as the result of her relationship with this William. Craig had always impressed her as a sweet, very nice boy for her. But now she was a grown woman and must make her own decisions in her life, and she would not offer any opinions on her private life. And she would always care for her and now her coming baby.

As Amanda said good day to her she'd kissed her and Delia had kissed her too, Delia was so, so good and she'd be excellent for her coming baby too. As she was now alone in her room, she was so looking forward to her time with William.

That late afternoon as she rested and fell asleep and dreamed of a hot, bright day in some smoking fields she didn't know. She saw blue- and gray-coated soldiers screaming in rage and agony and fright charging each other and bayonetting each other. Cannonballs tore apart living men, leaving dismembered bloody body parts. This was Gettysburg in Pennsylvania where her William had died. She didn't see him anywhere as she had before in her long-ago dream of Gettysburg, but she saw bloody piles of gruesome wounded bodies.

The dead were at least silent being beyond pain now, but the living wounded were crying in sheer agony. She felt her ears would burst with the cries. Then she saw phantom, ghostly forms rising from the bodies and roaming the battlefields, too, looking so lost and bewildered, lots and lots of them. So many on both sides had died at Gettysburg.

The Civil War at least had ended the great evil of black slavery, but it was at such a horrific price. She, while appalled at this historical nightmare on her part and crying in her sleep, that because slavery was such a terrible evil on its innocent victims, perhaps the horrors and many, many fratricidal deaths of the civil war was the horrific divine retribution, the karma for the awful way the young America had treated its slaves and Indians, too, for that matter. The land of the free and the brave had very bad beginnings for its nonwhite peoples, and it seemed the Civil War was karma due from a deadly and just heaven.

Truly, if God knew if even a sparrow fell dead on earth, he knew all the horrors slavery for blacks and genocide of the Indians needed a terrible justice for a nation steeped in such sins.

Then Amanda, still full of horror, woke up with Rita rapping at her bedroom door with her dinner. Ah, despite what she'd seen in her nightmare and how it had disturbed her, she was hungry. As the months had gone by, she found her appetite beginning to grow. Well, she was pregnant and now eating for two.

And she was so looking forward to seeing William tonight, too. Yes, he could visit her every day now and definitely every night, too. She'd assuage the horror with the coming raptures with William. His lovemaking could and would make her feel immensely happy and restore her equanimity. Yes, the Civil War was horrific, but perhaps a just punishment from heaven upon an iniquitous nation, but it was long past. Now was the time for peace and even rapture for her. She felt she would be truly happy now no matter what.

That evening her lawyer, Mr. Jack Dearborne, called her and said he'd seen Craig Weston that afternoon. "Craig had been in tears and had said he didn't want to separate or divorce but felt compelled to now. He'd made a wild claim that he had caught you having adulterous relations with another man on the new honeymoon and that said man had tried to kill him after he'd struck you. He said the only reason he's still alive was because you interceded. But with this, the real threat to his life and catching you in flagrante delicto on the honeymoon, the marriage is over. He will not contest it and for the sake of his love for you will not mention the adultery in court. Upon seeing the pictures of your bruises, I'm sure the judge will quickly grant your divorce."

"Good," she said, "and the sooner, the better. But tell him from me good luck in his studies from me. But I definitely do not wish to see him again. Now or ever, except in a courtroom for the divorce. Whatever was between us is finished, is over, period. Thank you, Mr. Dearborne for your services. As I said, keep this divorce as much as you can out of the papers."

"Well," her lawyer equivocated, "your very recent wedding was a cause celebre in this city. Word will inevitably leak out, and at least among the gilded set in this city, everyone knows everyone her or is somehow related, from the highest to the lowest, so even if it's somehow kept out of the papers, word will, unfortunately from your perspective, get out. And I'll tell you now, the way this city is, they'll pity Craig more than you in this. That's just the way good old Southerners think. They still respect marriage vows and all."

"Hey, whatever they say, we know who abused me physically. Let them say what they will. But with this divorce, he'll go his way and I'll go mine and that's how I want it, period. Mr. Dearborne, you have done your job well and I'll thank you with a fat little check for your services today. Thank you for your services. You are one of the best lawyers in this fabled city. Tell me later if I must appear in court or not for the judge's verdict. Though I think, thanks to you it'll be a fait accompli as the French say. Thank you, sir."

And with that, she gratefully hung up. Goodbye, Craig Weston, goodbye. Now it was just her and Wiliam, period.

Within two weeks, both she and Craig appeared before a civil affairs judge in Richmond. He asked them if they both agreed to this divorce so early in their new marriage because of irreconcilable differences.

Craig looked at Amanda and said, "I do not wish for this divorce, but if she does, that's it, I guess. I won't contest it at all if this is her will."

"And why shouldn't it be after the way you treated me on our wedding night of all nights, Craig? And the pictures prove it! All right because the pictures my lawyer took corroborate my story!"

Craig just looked at her and said, "So you no longer love me at all, do you?"

"I guess not, Craig. I think our marriage was a bad mistake. But I harbor no ill feelings. You just live your life and I'll live mine."

"And when the baby comes, will I get to ever visit it at all, Amanda?"

"We'll see how I feel then, Craig. That's still a ways off."

The judge, a Harry Stone, looked directly at Amanda and said, "Look, Ms. Amanda Mannon, I don't like that. To deny a father visiting his own baby is wrong. If there was some wrongdoing on his part which destroyed your affections for him, I will say he is still not a bad person. He's a law student with stellar grades and will probably be a good lawyer someday. He's never been in trouble of any sort before and apparently, his heart is misapplied in this case, still loves you. To deny him visiting rights to his own child is a punishment he does not deserve. When this child is finally born, I think you should reconsider how you feel now. Your child would get a loving father, anyway."

"Your Honor, I grew up never knowing my father and my mother never loved me or was at all concerned about me and I turned out just fine now! The strong always make it!"

"That remains to be seen, Miss Amanda Mannon. Don't recreate your parents' neglect and mistakes on a new generation of Mannons and Westons. If I may interject, I know of both your and now your former husband's families, good old families of Richmond's finest. I was happy when I learned of your high society wedding. I think this whole divorce is a shame and a mistake on your part. But you may feel you have your reasons and you may. But this young man, I can tell from his face and demeanor is a very fine, very loving man, but I hold no woman in marriage to a man whom she no longer loves or wants. I decree this marriage dissolved. I sincerely hope, Amanda Mannon, you never have any regrets over your actions this day, but you very well might at some point. But you are hereby the mistress entirely of your own fate. Young man, Mr. Weston, go back to school and become what I know you can be, one of Richmond's most brilliant and most capable lawyer of a league of great lawyers the city of Richmond is known for. And, young lady, I hope in the future, you and your coming child's future, I hope you never cause another person the pain you've caused this young man whose only mistake was to love you unwisely, in my opinion, and too unwell. This court is now over."

And he struck his gavel down, and the loud banging was heard all throughout the very still courtroom. Amanda looked furiously at the judge. That man had dressed her down in front of the whole court.

Her lawyer had not prepared her for this. All sympathy should have been for her, the abused young wife as she made herself out to be, not for Craig Weston. Ah, men, were any of them, even the handsomest ones ever worth it, the living and the dead?

Well, she smiled to herself, she suddenly knew one dead man who was most decidedly worth it, William. What a good laugh they'd have together tonight when she told him what the judge had said. Well, after all, she had to give credit to the judge. He'd seen through her ploy. Craig was really no abusive husband.

She'd just used his spontaneous violence to her, which in her heart of hearts, she knew was really justified with her making love to William in front of him and she had tried to use against him. Of course, if poor Craig had said that he had seen his beautiful young wife making love to a ghost, they would have locked him up in some looney-bin somewhere. So this was it.

Craig suddenly moved from his seat and went over to her. She looked at him and suddenly felt a little bit bad for him.

"Goodbye, Craig, I guess. You live your life and I'll live mine. Go back to college and become like the judge said, a brilliant lawyer."

"Goodye for now, Amanda. But I will be seeing you in the future when our child's born."

"Oh, Craig, it's wrong and stupid of you to keep on loving me when I've deeply hurt you so. But we can't be together again. Our marriage is dissolved and so is whatever legal hold you have over me. Later on, I might let you visit your child. But now just go back to your life as I'll go back to mine."

"Yes, Amanda," he said simply, smiling a bit crookedly at her, "I'll go back to school and my life and you'll go back to William, won't you? You're obsessed with him, aren't you? I think you married me just to give the baby a name!"

"Well, I had to do something, didn't I? And I did tell you of him before we even got married and I swear I said I'd always have William. You should have been a little reasonable, Craig, boy. If you had only let me have William, too, I could have given you everything in the world!"

"Amanda," Craig said, a ghastly hurt look on his face, "give it up, please, give it up, this sick, twisted, unnatural love of yours. It'll destroy you utterly someday!"

And then he turned his back on her and she nearly screamed at his now retreating form, "Oh, Craig, as I once said, get with the times. You are so prissy bourgeois. I'm glad we're no longer married!"

And then she turned to Mr. Dearborne, who'd been strangely silent when Judge Stone had been publicly dressing her down.

"Well, Amanda, you got what you wanted, a divorce and a name for your coming baby. I should have warned you about old Judge Stone. He has great insight and is uncannily bright. It seems he caught you out."

"Well, so he did, so what? I have what I want, Mr. Dearborne, I have what I want and tha's all that counts in my books."

"I guess so, Amanda. At any rate, I, for one, am happy this case is over."

"So am I, Mr.Dearborne, so am I."

And so Amanda walked ahead of Mr. Dearborne to what she felt entirely would be a wonderful new life without Craig. A life full of William, William, William. Outside the courthouse, the sun was beaming, and she felt she was walking into a wonderful new future.

And so, after the divorce, life went on quite pleasantly for Amanda. She, after all, had William to love. They made love two or three times a day and night now that daylight wouldn't banish William from her. Their love-making was ecstatic, thrilling, delicious, indeed, delectable to all her senses.

She mostly stayed on her suite of rooms reading, watching Tv and awaiting the materialization of her ghost-lover. Sometimes, Delia sat with her and talked to her about anything and everything, from Amanda's bleak childhood in which Amanda knew Delia was the total mother surrogate and only source of nurture and maternal love.

But when Amanda said she sensed William coming so Delia must leave her, Amanda's rooms for a while, a hurt look would come over her face and she'd quickly scuttle herself out of the rooms.

Sometimes, Amanda heard Delia praying for her, Amanda's soul because of what she was doing with William, but it only caused Amanda to laugh to herself a bit. How could something as wonderful and pleasurable as William and his divine love-making skills be sinful or immoral?

Didn't Delia understand that if it had only been possible, now in her divorced state, she would have married William in a heartbeat! But so far anyway, she knew of no religion or priest or minister there who would marry a woman and her ghost lover!

So what, though?

She was the mistress of the Mannon fortune and mansion now and her staff of her maids and male servants did her bidding very well. They didn't know exactly what was going on in her suite of rooms daily and nightly, but she could tell that they suspected something sinister was afoot.

But really, Amanda was a generous and kindly employer and their jobs depended on their obedience to her and their discretion, too. But in fact, Amanda only went out for her monthly visits to her obstetrician, and he seemed pleased with her pregnancy's progress and also said the baby seemed to be due in early May.

So she ate well, took the prescribed vitamins and minerals, and took daily walks for light aerobic exercise her doctor had recommended in the still beautiful gardens around the house.

It being now mid-fall, the roses were mostly gone, but some other flowers were still blooming. There were a couple of beautiful jasmine bushes that were still blooming and how fragrant they were. And Delia now made her some raspberry tea to strengthen her uterus for the coming birth.

Delia had said she felt she would bear a boy and Amanda looked so forward to it. She'd begun knitting the baby some baby clothes and baby socks, and next month, she would buy a layette and basinet and baby stroller for her coming child. Her figure filled out a bit and her complexion was a rosy pink she looked and felt the picture of health and she'd only had a little of that nasty morning sickness, and now that she was past the first trimester, there would be none.

Delia had told her that when her mother had discovered herself pregnant with her, she had asked Delia for some old herbal brew to get rid of her pregnancy.

But Delia had refused and said to her that having a baby was God's business with a woman and if she didn't want this baby, she, Delia, would take good care of it and Aurelia had gone off in a huff.

"So, Delia, you saved me from my so mean mother even before I was born, didn't you!"

"Indeed I did, Amanda."

"And you've been saving me ever since."

"Indeed I have, Mandy, indeed I have. But now there is one black thing it seems I can't save you from."

"Oh, Delia, never mind about me and William. I'm a grown woman and know what I'm doing!"

"But it's wrong, it's so wrong this mingling of the living and the dead!"

"Delia, shut up about that now! Let me live my own life and just help me with this baby!"

Delia looked very mortified and hurt by her and said, "Yes," and did not speak again to her for the rest of the day.

But Amanda could hear Delia praying for her soul long into the night in her bedroom adjacent to her own.

For a few moments, she felt distinctly uncomfortable with a little guilt.

But then, the so handsome William materialized and soon they were making that estatic love and she quite forgot about Delia and her prayers.

As the fall progressed and the leaves turned all those wonderful magical colors and the days grew colder, too, Amanda still took her walks in the now fading garden. Everything was now dormant for the coming winter, but to her, the garden was still beautiful only in a different way.

Certainly, the two gardeners Jame and Nick, older men who'd been the gardeners for years were very conservative about the many fallen leaves. Then come mid-November, she got a shock from some unexpected news. Her lawyer called her and told her her old, eccentric Great-Aunt Eliza had been found dead in her house in Gettysburg, Pennsylvania. He said she'd apparently had some sort of a seizure or even mild sudden epileptic fit, and during it, her tongue had logged in her throat and had suffocated her to death.

The death, while a little grisly, looked totally natural, especially for a woman her age. The woman's lawyer had contacted him. In her will, she had wanted no funeral, just a hasty burial in an old almost decayed graveyard where a lot of Confederate soldiers had been buried from Gettysburg.

Well, Amanda thought, sly old girl, Aunt Eliza could not give up her soldiers even in death. She really didn't know about a heaven or hell but felt her great-aunt was lost while still alive and was now one lost dead. Buried near, undoubtedly, the dessicated remains of the soldiers whose ghosts had pleased her for so very long.

Then she thought of her late aunt's ghostly lovers. Where would they go now? Would they still haunt her now empty old mansion or just casually haunt the grounds of Gettysburg? She didn't know the answer to that, but she was just glad she had her one Confederate, William.

Then her lawyer, Mr. Lovejoy, said he'd been sent a copy of her great-aunt's will and in which, for some strange reason Amanda couldn't fathom, had been left the solid bulk of Eliza's really considerable inheritance of around three million dollars and the old mansion the old girl had lived long, lonely years. And the funny thing was, Aunt Eliza had her will changed the last time she'd seen Aunt Eliza for her Aunt Lavinia's funeral.

But she really hadn't liked or loved this strange great-aunt. In fact, she found her strange and repelling with her tales of many ghostly lovers.

In fact, William had been originally sent to her by the bizarre Great-Aunt Eliza. But why did the old bat leave her her entire fortune?

Well, she'd have to break her routine and have the chauffeur drive her into Richmond to see Mr. Dearborne to settle this will and new development in her life! What had the old lady been getting at by such a bounteous favor? True, her aunt Eliza had been quite glad that she herself was a mediumistic witch like herself and the fact that she had freely taken the handsome William for her lover. But that was where the similarity ended.

She would never have a whole flock of ghostly lovers and do her depraved games almost in the public eye. What did the old witch mean by this? That she was her natural heir, not only of her powers but now her wealth, too?

It was all so strange! It's not like she really needed the money. But now that she was pregnant, that meant that much more for her coming child. She was glad of that. And she wouldn't be totally selfish with it either. She'd give some good amounts to a few charities she favored. Mostly charities that helped poor and disadvantaged children mostly in America.

She knew that despite being an affluent country, there were many children who daily faced hardship, hunger, and sexual and physical abuse and neglect. Hell, her own stepfather had taken foul advantage of her when she was no more than fifteen and then had tried to kill her for having discovered her mother's decayed remains in the cellar.

Sometimes when she was bored of reading and listening to some light, classical music, wondered for long, still periods how she would have developed if her mother had actually loved her and there were a loving father in the picture too.

But how well she knew herself or so she thought. Whatever her faults and idiosyncrasies she felt that many of them were inborn, probably genetic like her occult powers, a bad seed coming from some twisted roots. Had she not had more than a hand in her own fall and seduction by her stepfather? What kind of fifteen-year-old girl did that?

Well, though, thank god she'd had Delia raising her and acting as a good mother surrogate. But her faults and maladjustments were there, she had never really been a child. When her mother had neglected her so, she had not really minded but had quickly learned not to give or receive any love from such a woman. It didn't in the end greatly mater to her, anyway. The past was the past, and now she was very rich and about to get even richer.

Obviously, it wasn't that she was unaware that there was or supposed to be a spiritual side to life, but how well she knew that in this world, money was the true and basically only real power on earth, despite all the Christian platitudes the south was so filled with.

So Tuesday, the next day, she had the chauffeur drive her into her lawyer's office in Richmond.

"Always a pleasure to see you and to do business with you, Ms. Amanda Mannon, or would you still prefer Ms. Weston still?"

Mr. Dearborne remarked to her, smiling most sardonically.

"Ms. Mannon will do nicely, and you knew that. You helped me get the divorce, after all. Now what's this business about Aunt Eliza's will?"

"Just this, Amanda," the lawyer took out a legal-looking document and laid it before him on his heavy metal and shining oakwood desk.

He began reading from it to a now sitting Amanda before him, "I, Eliza Mannon, being of sound mind and now not so sound body, do bequeath my fund of three and a half million dollars to her as my one and only heir. I also bequeath to her my house in Gettysburg, not to sell it but to modernize it as she will. I feel that this house will be, as it has been for me, a refuge in a long dark night that she may live in as she will and bequeath also to whatever heirs of her body may come."

"I wonder," said Amanda aloud to the lawyer and to herself, too, "if she'd heard somehow I'd married and divorced Craig and was pregnant."

"It's possible, I suppose."

"Why, did you and she talk on the phone or write each other?" the lawyer asked her as if such actions were mortal impossibilities in this world, anyway, as if he could not imagine anyone calling or writing to Aunt Eliza Mannon.

"No, I did not, Mr. Dearborne, but a woman like Aunt Eliza had her own way of knowing such a thing and many others. I think I'll refurbish her house. I've heard it's a big wreck of a mansion now. Who knows, as it's near Gettysburg and there are lots of civil war tourists in the area, I might make it a historical bed and breakfast establishment or something."

But even as she said this, she knew she was speaking nonsense. The mansion was haunted by the Civil War ghosts her aunt had amused herself with. No, she'd just fix up the place and see what else happened.

Then as if coming from a light trance, she said to the lawyer, "Look, sir, I have a list of some worthy charities I want to give money to from my now enriched estate. Will you help me do that?"

So she gave Mr. Dearborne the list and signed her aunt's will and other many legal documents, and within a few days, her bank accounts would be considerably richer and she would be the owner of Aunt Eliza's ranshackle mansion in Pennsylvania. Well, what else would now transpire?

Where would her great-aunt's collection of ghost lovers, if she could call them that, go to?

Something told her that they wouldn't be satisfied now with just roaming and haunting the grounds of Gettysburg. Oh, well, time would tell now but she had a slightly ominous feeling about it all. And as she left the lawyer's office, she felt some new happiness she was richer, but she also knew inside this wasn't the end of her bizarre Aunt Eliza's legacy to her at all, no, it wasn't the end at all.

That night, after William had materialized and rather violently and frantically made love to her which she'd enjoyed very much, and both being naked, she dreamily fell asleep in his arms.

As she was drifting off to sleep, she kissed William feverishly all over and said to him, "William, I am alive and you are a ghost, but I believe the best physical lover any woman could wish for!"

"But tell me, and you being now dead for a long, long time, what is it really like?"

"Well," he said, smiling at her, "there is no more pain unless we somehow choose to relive our often horrible deaths or wish pain on ourselves for the supposed wrongs we committed when alive. Or unless we were so bad in life, we wind up in hell, but I don't want to talk about that subject. But usually, there is no more hunger or thirst also. But if we choose to eat, one can just think of the particular dish and it suddenly appears before us and we think of silverware and that appears also and we eat. I suppose we enjoy it. Ghost food tastes even better than real food for the living because the food we materialize for ourselves is a dream of the best food we ever had on earth. Of course, there is a difference between spirits who, at their deaths, ascent into the light and spirits like me and my comrades who died in battle with me. We chose to stay on the earth plane."

"But why, why choose to be earth-bound at all?"

"Some of us because of the horrible deaths we died and could not just slough off the pain of it and we were stuck. And some of us were too angry with our young lives being so cut short and we chose to stay to seek possible vengeance however we might. And some, I suppose, don't accept that they're really dead. So we are here?"

"You know my aunt Eliza died, don't you?"

"Of course, I do. Her death was accidental but natural. She was very old."

"What will happen to the soldier ghosts she, ah, entertained?"

"I was hoping some of my friends in the spirit could come here."

"No, William, no! I forbid it! It's nice with just you and me here. I don't need any more ghosts here except my guide, Lily!"

"Oh, come on, broaden your horizons, you could learn more things from my dead soldier friends. Your powers would grow considerably to the point where you'd be a far more powerful witch than your aunt Eliza! Believe me, the dead can teach you far more than the living. And you didn't object to my friends being here to attack those Ku Klux Klan men who were going to attack you and burn your house down. They came and helped you!"

"No, William, please!" And she pounded against his hairy chest, and he laughed at her and then, as if to punish her, disappeared!

Oh, well, she had hoped that she could fall asleep in his strong arms. Well, maybe she shouldn't have said no to him in this. What were some more ghosts around her? She knew they could be protective of her and hers.

They had probably used their etheric energy to assist her aunt Eliza become a really powerful witch that she was! Everything was, after all, energy. With that thought, without his diving, wonderful body caressing hers, she fell quickly and deeply asleep. And then she had a very strange but interesting dream.

In the dream, she was again Katy, that Civil War girl, and she was in William's arms in that meadow they used as a trysting place. She was naked and so was he, and ecstasy ran through her body and her veins tingled with wild waves of molten passion.

And then something felt different and the face and body upon her changed, morphed into a rather handsome, rugged-looking blond man, and she felt waves of ecstasy coursing through her, but she wanted to stop and scream that it wasn't William but a complete stranger.

And then she noticed that there were several naked young men standing around her body looking longingly and then the face and body again changed, morphed again into this time William's, and she cried and kissed him, and then as she was kissing him, his face changed again into her handsome, evil, murderous stepfather from when she was just fifteen!

In the dream, she screamed and began scratching him and pounding his leering still undeniably handsome face. And then the men standing around her were laughing and leering too.

And suddenly she woke up and noticed that her nightgown was not just lying by her body but torn and shredded and her sheets had become all tangled and a few of the satin pillows were on the floor.

She gasped and ran into the bathroom and looked at herself in the full-length mirror. Her hair was all disheveled, and there were scratches and black and blue marks on her body and neck and shoulders and even some on her face!

What the hell had happened in that dream turned into erotic nightmare?

William was involved and possibly behind it, and he owed her quite an explanation!

What was she to do now? As if she herself sensed or felt something was very wrong, Delia opened her bedroom door and came in still dressed in her blue cotton nightgown and bathrobe. She cried, "Amanda, is something wrong? I's had the most awful bad dream about you last night! Is you all right?"

Then Delia waddled her way to the bathroom and beheld Amanda's bruised body. She appeared silently shocked for around five minutes, then erupted at her, "Is this what this William has done to you? Get rid of him now! You is pregnant now and treatment like that could make you lose the baby! What happened?"

"I don't know exactly, Delia. I had a nightmare last night. I dreamt last night he was violently making love to me and then he changed into someone else. And then there were three or four of his dead rebel friends of his around me. And last night, I even saw Ted, my awful, murdering stepfather making love to me too!"

She went to Delia who, horrified, moved a little away from her and then embraced her and began saying, "This is what comes of your fooling around with the dead! And with your aunt Eliza dying now, some of her ghosts could come here now!"

"Delia, you're right! What am I to do now?"

With that, Amanda virtually dissolved into tears and Delia moved her to her messed-up bed. Delia went back to the bathroom and got some face cloths with soap and a basin full of hot, steaming water and then began to clean Amanda up, being gentle on her bruises.

Later she made up Amanda's bed with fresh satin sheets and ordered up breakfast for Amanda, and served her breakfast in bed.

After breakfast, Amanda said to Delia, "Maybe I just had nightmares last night, and with my body contortions, I just bruised myself!"

To which Delia laughed a little scornfully and said, "Ha! Stop fooling yaself! This was William and maybe more than William, maybe a few of his friends, too! The dead are always hungry for the living and any bits of life they can get from them!"

"Oh, Delia, he and I had a quarrel. He was angry! But he's never been this way before with me! And years ago, when that awful judge and his KKK buddies tried to burn me out of Richmond, William and his ghostly friends attacked them and defeated them!"

Delia just looked at her very penetratingly and said, "Please tell me you'll use whatever powers you have to drive this William and his friends away from here back to where he belongs, Gettysburg or whatever he and his friends will stay away from you and this house! I mean it, promise me, Amanda!"

Amanda shook her golden head and said, "The other ghosts, yes, but I think I still love him Delia, though I know he can be violent, even dangerous, Delia! But when he makes love to me I feel such pleasure, fireworks go off in me!"

"Then you is a fool of a young woman, Amanda Mannon! I's not goin to help you anymore! If William stays here, he'll get his other ghostly friends here, too! Now that your Aunt Eliza is dead and her ghosts who were so used to the ways of the flesh, her tired, wrinkled flesh, anyways, with her will come here to see if they can fool with you like they fooled with that crazy old lady! Do you understand me! I'll leave you now, and I'll be in my own room praying for God himself to intervene to save you and ya baby! Iffins you need anything calls one of the other maids, Rita or Margaret or someone else. I's can only help someone if they's want to help theirself first!"

Then Delia walked up in a huff and went straight to her rooms to do what she'd said, pray and pray! But she didn't understand, she could no more banish William from her than she could cut her own heart in half. Surely, he had some explanation for her!

Like in her dream/nightmare of last night, had she been sexually possessed by other ghosts as she thought she saw and felt or had it been William all along just changing from and shape to fool her?

No, she felt, the other spirits who'd been on her sexually had felt too real to be just fragments of her mind, and how about the ghosts of other what seemed like other Confederate soldiers around her last night as if awaiting their turn with her?

She deserved an explanation. She called downstairs and asked one of the maids to bring up her lunch around 12:30 p.m. to knock on her door when she did. She put her radio on to some light, sweet classical music by Tchaikovsky, one of her very favorites.

Later, after she'd finished a most delicious lunch of pan-fried beef liver her doctor had her eat once every two weeks to build up her iron and other vitamin reserves for her pregnancy and creamed vegetables and a strawberry torte for dessert, she settled down to reading. She just knew William would come by in the evening for her and she would really, really grill him as to what exactly had happened last night.

Time passed, she fell asleep, she really was so tired. The lower part of her body, where some bruises were, pained her a little. But in her pregnant state, she didn't dare even take an aspirin for the pain. No, no medication or drug was safe for fear of how it might affect the baby. But she was awfully tired from last night. Not just physically tired but psychically, spiritually tired also.

Like raw life itself had eaten her whole in its savage maw and spit her out, too. She had a dream she was walking in a rather familiar field near a little trebly stream. She looked at her dress and it was the period-piece blue dress she wore in her dreams when she'd been the girl Katy, William's sweetheart.

Thinking of William, where was he now? He usually visited her now in her dreams as he was in the Civil War. And then, before her eyes, the scenery changed and she could now smell gunpowder and the nauseous sulfurous smell of exploded cannonballs.

She heard cries of torment and agony. She saw a dried yellow field strewn with dead and horribly wounded men and horses who were dismembered, torn apart by guns, cannonballs, and bayonets.

Her breath choked in her throat as she inhaled the stench of death and rot and decay and excretion, too. It was the horrid stench of a very carnal house. And then she came upon William or what was left of him.

Blood was still pouring out of savage bayonet wounds in his chest and lower body. Some of his intestines were visibly trailing from an abdominal wound and still he breathed, laboriously as if his each stentorious breath would be his last. His blue eyes were glassy, glazed, almost opaque. And then his eyes alighted on her and he screamed aloud in his agony, "Katy, Katy, I was praying and praying you'd come! Katy, Katy I love you!"

Then he cried aloud in his agony and then in a deeply gravelly voice gasped, "And we will never, never be apart, Katy, my heart, never be apart, ever!"

And she knelt down over him, even though the battle-grime and dirt besmirched her and kissed him on his expiring lips as the blood of life oozed from them. His drops of scarlet blood tasted bitter, copperish, somehow. And she said, "Never, never be apart, William, we will always be together forever and ever."

Then the breath of life departed from him and she looked into his now sightless, dead blue eyes and, as tenderly as possible, closed them.

Then she saw a wispy form emerge from his still, cooling body and then she saw many, many other translucent forms floating neat. the still bodies they once owned and she wanted to follow William's spirit and she tried to touch and hold him. but her hands went through his wispy, ethereal spirit.

She wailed aloud at him and all the ghosts wandering lost on the last battlefield of Gettysburg and she keened and wailed like an Irish banshee of her heritage and she said, "Forever, William, I swear it. From one lifetime to another, forever, William, together, forever! I swear by heaven and hell, forever!"

Her banshee wail echoed almost thunderously on the bloody battlefield, and she suddenly awoke in her bed as Amanda Mannon. She had been screaming and sobbing apparently in her sleep!

Well, that explained it, she had made a death vow to William to be with him forever and even come heaven or hell on a battlefield of massacre, blood, death, and madness. Somehow they had been holy or unholy vows, and God or perhaps the devil had heard them and would forever see that she carried them out, to follow William through the endless eddy and flow of lifetime and deathtime, birth and rebirth again and again and again, oh, when did it all end?

This was their fate now, their destiny, forever and ever and no one and nothing could ever stop it!

In the room's dim beginning morning light, she saw a shimmer of glittering white light. She knew it as her William. A strong, masculine figure materialized in the light, and it was the nude, pale, beautiful figure of William fully erect.

She nearly gasped at his startling male beauty as she always did when she saw him naked. Finally, when he'd fully solidified, he walked to her bed and lay down beside her. She kissed him on his lips and all over and she said, "I dreamt a very interesting dream of you, William."

"What you saw and experienced was no dream as Katy, my Katy, but as an experience from your lifetime as Katy."

"You mean I, we, made that vow to be together always, lifetime after lifetime forever and ever?"

"Yes, we did and so we shall be!"

And then he was kissing her roughly as his skillful hands were caressing her. In a moment, she was naked, and he was kissing her breasts with her fully erect red nipples as he began biting them tenderly. Wave after wave of sheer physical ecstasy coursed through her breasts, rippling through her whole body.

His rough kisses drove her utterly wild, and as he entered her, she exploded in a total nova of orgasmic rapture and ecstasy. This time, there was nothing tender in his love-making. It was rough, almost brutal, like he was trying to rape or ravish and conquer her. But she was all too willing to be so assailed and was panting with the passionate delirium he put her into.

Finally, he heaved triumphantly in her and yelled, "Oh, god and the devil," and she climaxed too and shuddered under him as the rapture slowly faded from her body and senses.

"So it's settled then now, you will allow my dead friends and brothers from the fields of Gettysburg to stay here at this house as they will!"

And almost without thinking, she said, "Yes, William, yes to everything you say. But see that they don't manifest to any of my staff or Delia. That's all I ask. They'd be frightened and leave if they did."

"I'll try to keep them in check. I will say they had great fun and tasted mortal life again with your aunt Eliza."

"That may be, William, but I'm not another Eliza. See that they keep out of my dreams and person. I want only you, William, only you in keeping with those hallowed vows we made so long ago. You and no one else in life and death!"

"In life and death, Amanda," he said roughly kissing her and beginning to more gently make love to her again.

Later that night, in her own rooms, Delia woke up at 1:00 a.m. and knew, just knew something was very wrong. She felt as if she were being watched. She turned on her bedroom lamp by her bed and looked around and couldn't see anyone. She just knew someone or even two or more beings were watching her with perhaps more than a hint of malice.

She did what she normally did in those rare moments of her life when she felt she was confronting something supernatural. That had happened more than a few times when she'd lived with Amanda's late mother and her husband. She'd known almost from the girl's birth that Amanda was born knowing and seeing fully the things beyond the veil of life and death and that she, Delia, could certainly sense them and sometimes see them too.

She really didn't want such a gift as it could be so frightening, but she did what she usually did when the situation called for it. She grabbed her battered old King James Bible and earnestly prayed verses and prayers from it. But now in her bedroom adjoining Amanda's suite of rooms, the old Bible and its prayers and psalms wasn't working at all.

She felt a wave of energy, a dark, negative energy was focusing on her. Suddenly, she was seeing the ghosts before her bed materialize. There were three of them. Rough-looking men in gray Confederate uniforms, torn and bloodied. The first male ghost ahead of the other two was blond and had a bronze, disheveled beard. His b ue eyes looked at her hungrily, "Why, what do we have here, a soft nigga bitch. Dark flesh is the easiest to plow. Nigga bitch, you gonna be honored by three boys in gray. God save the South!"

Her fear galvanized and froze her as the three ghosts approached and she screamed at them, "Don't filth like you dare touch me, go back to Gettysburg where you belong!"

"Better still, go back to hell where you really belong!"

The blond ghost struck her hard across the face. The blow was very strong from a ghost.

Her lower lip was in fact bleeding and then she felt her nightgown being torn and she fought him, then the three Confederate ghosts converged on her and she was stripped naked, her large, sagging, pendulous black breasts roughly fondled and bitten and she screamed and cried futilely into the darkness as her bedside lamp fell to the floor and broke.

She was in pitch darkness and violated all over again and again and again by the malignant force of three previously been sated by the ageing flesh of Aunt Eliza in Gettysburg.

She screamed long, hard, and futilely in the darkness and asked, imploringly, "Oh where, is you, God, Jesus, where are you?"

She mercifully lost her breath and then lost all consciousness as the ghosts violated her now numb body again and again and again!

They finally left her and disappeared. She was alive, but, mercifully, in unfeeling shock. When she finally awoke in the morning light, her fear and humiliation changed into quite another emotion, pure, primal rage! She hurriedly got dressed in yesterday's lavender dress and ran down to see Amanda and force her to give up these fucking ghosts for good!

Amanda awoke alone in her bed. Where had William gone? There was a harsh pounding at her bedroom door and Delia screaming at her to open up! Why, what was this? Whatever was wrong? Why did Delia sound so frantic and angry?

Amanda swiftly got up and opened the door. She was amazed to see Delia looking battered and bruised from head to toe and a furious expression on her face!

"Delia, Delia, what happened to you? Did you fall downstairs or something?"

"Naw, I didn't fall downstairs! I was raped by three of ya William's ghost friends in gray! They came upon me by surprise and took me again and again!"

"Now I wants ya to swear on this here Bible you will send this ghost William and all his rebel buddies back to Gettysburg or even better, back to hell where ya know they belong!"

Amanda looked frozen with shock and said, "Hey, Delia, William did not hurt you. It was his ghost friends who did that! I'll try my best to send his friends back but not my William. Delia, he had no hand in what happened to you!"

"Oh, you're still sticking wid this fucking William, are you even with what just happened to me! Listen, this afternoon I'll be packed up! Please pay me my wages and have the chauffeur drive me back to my old place at Bourbonville! I'll never come here again! This is too much and I'm telling you these damn spooks are fucking dangerous! You think this William would protect you from his friends! Listen, my dead granny told me that in the war between the states, the rebel men would often rape any black woman they could find when they didn't have their whores around! And I will not be put in this position again here!"

Amanda began to cry, "Oh, Delia, you're really leaving me? Well, I can't blame you with what's just happened to you! Come into my room and I'll ring Rita up to bring us rolls and tea or something. Just calm down, honey!"

"I ain't taking no tea with you to have some kind of tea party with what's just happened to me! If you can't choose me over this William and his rebel buddies, I'm leaving you! I guess I still loves you and I will pray for you and your coming baby's protection. But I's clearing out of here today! You love these raping, violent ghosts so much over me, here, you deal wid them, I'm leaving!"

And so, no matter how much Amanda cried and pleaded with Delia, Delia was adamant about leaving that very day.

Finally, she packed up, and after, Amanda wrote her a big check for her which was a lot more than her current wages, but Amanda didn't want Delia to lack for anything.

Her life would be far lonelier, more desolate without Delia, but God help her, she would not give up William, her William. Later that day, as a packed and formally dressed Delia stood before her with her packed suitcase and the check in her pocketbook, Amanda kissed her goodbye and Delia kissed her back!

Delia said to her, "If only you had stayed married to old Craig Weston. He was a real good young man. He would have made you see sense about this William!"

"That's neither here nor there now, Delia, Craig and I are all over with now, I don't love him like I do William and that's that! Goodbye, Delia. Be careful, please. Bourbonville can be a rough place!"

"You're talking to a woman who's just been raped by very strong rebel ghosts here! Don't talk to me of dangerous places! This here place is dangerous enough right now, and god help you if William and his friends turn on you as they very well could! These men in life were rough, dangerous men and are now even more so in death! Either banish them from here now if you can or leave with me now! We can live together again, just no ghosts, okay?"

"Delia," said Amanda, kissing Delia softly, "you know I do love and care for you, but I cannot banish William from me now or ever! You call me once you settle and if there's anything you ever need!"

"What I needs is you being away from this ghost craziness and you're being safe! But that's not to be, I guess! Goodbye, Amanda, I will pray for you and your coming baby!"

They kissed and Delia left and was driven by Henrique the chauffeur to Bourbonville.

Bourbonville was still a very rough slum area of Richmond, but to old Delia's mind, it was a lot safer for her personally than the mansion she'd just left.

That evening, when William materialized by her bed. Amanda was very angry with him.

"You know three of your rebel friends who came with you from Aunt Eliza's mansion sexually assaulted Delia with great violence, I saw her bruises! I'm going to send all of your friends back to Gettysburg soon! Delia's just left and won't be back! I never thought these ghosts could be that vicious and dangerous!"

William looked angrily back at her and said, "No, you will not send my friends, comrades-in-arms I died with back to Gettysburg! I don't care what happened to your Delia! She was just an interfering and uppity old nigger wench!"

"William," she screamed at him, "she was beaten and raped by three of your Confederate brothers! If you can't see what is wrong with that, then I might just banish you,= too again!"

William instantly struck her hard across the face! He screamed at her furiously, "That's the trouble with you modern women of this age and day! You think you're your husbands and men's equals! You are not! A wife or woman have to obey their husbands in all things! And Delia was just an interfering old nigger bitch who needed her lessons in obedience to white masters taught severely! In my day, the old nigger bitch would have been strung up and whipped but good to teach her a lesson!"

"Get away from me, William!" screamed Amanda, holding the bruised side of her face where William had struck her hard.

"Get away now, Delia's right, you ghosts here are vicious and violent!"

Then before she could blink an eye, William was naked and jumped into her bed. He violently lay on top of her and began furiously penetrating her.

"You will obey me in all things! Bitch, golden whore who thinks herself greater than a man!" he kept muttering, though it was rough, violent, the grinding of their naked bodies together, felt good ripples of orgasmic pleasure coursed through her betraying body.

In some minutes, she orgasmed! But she thought, this wasn't love, it was rape, really. How could she have felt any pleasure in it at all? Then she remembered, the "Daddy" poem of the suicide Sylvia Plath of how women love a fascist, the brute's savage boot in the face, how women love a brutal bastard!

She now wondered if it was true. Then she saw three other ghosts float through the closed door of her bedroom. They, all three, wore tattered, bloodied gray uniforms and came to the side of her bed. They looked at her now ravished form like men who'd been out in a desert would look at a mirage of a deep blue waterfall!

She was suddenly really frightened and screamed, knowing their intent, "William, stop your friends, I don't want this!"

"Ha! You are a woman and a whore, my whore, you were meant to pleasure men! You must obey me in this! Pleasure my three brothers-in-arms!"

As the three ghosts converged on Amanda, she began keening and wailing and struggling against them! Good god, they were going to rape her like they'd raped Delia!

But she was pregnant she thought, almost as an afterthought, their rapist violence could cause her to miscarry the baby!

She screamed out to William, "William, I'm pregnant. Please don't let them do this to me!"

He smiled wickedly and said, "Pleasure my friends like your aunt Eliza did! Never mind about that there baby!"

And then the three were brutally on her. and she struggled, was hit. and slugged by the ghosts and then their erect members felt like stabbing ice-cold icicles inside her, ramming, ramming until she finally fainted dead away.

The last thing she remembered was thinking, *Dear God, please don't let them hurt my baby inside me!*

And then she passed totally out. It was an hour or so before the ghosts left her brutalized body, deeply unconscious now.

Finally, late in the morning, Rita awoke Amanda by tugging on her arm and speaking into her ears. She started awake, horrified as if the ghosts were there and waking her up for another round of sadistic violence.

But then she recognized Rita, her best maid, and Rita looked down at her and asked how she'd gotten those bruises on her body, face, and neck?

When Amanda, humiliated, didn't answer her, the maid went into the bathroom and came out with a plastic basin and some sweet-smelling soap and face cloths and began washing gently her face and those awful bruises.

She didn't speak to Rita. And when Rita suggested she call the police in to see her and get whoever so hurt her, she almost laughed in Rita's face at the idea. Ya, the police would really go searching for her rapists, three long-dead ghosts of Confederate soldiers! Oh, yes, if she ever let that out, she would be having her baby inside an insane asylum, and it would be taken away from her.

Craig would get full custody, and if she persisted in her story, she might remain in the asylum for life! So she didn't speak to Rita; she just cried and cried and wondered how her dream with William had turned now into such a twisted nightmare?

Three Months Later

IT WAS SPRINGTIME NOW, AND Amanda greatly appreciated the new golden warmth in the house, the big blue skies, and beautiful sunlight in the windows.

She badly wanted to walk about in the gardens of the mansion. But she didn't dare to. William and his ghostly friends might suddenly be taken with a hankering for her, even though she thought she looked grotesque with her very pregnant belly.

She was pretty near her due date in May. Miraculously, the sexual and physical abuse the ghosts put her through hadn't caused her to miscarry or deliver early and she felt the baby inside of her kicking and moving, so she was sure it was still alive.

Thank God, miracles did happen, she supposed. She'd stopped going outside of the house or seeing her doctors in Richmond. One really never knew when William and the ghosts would begin their erotic attack of her, and she didn't want the whole world to know she'd become another Aunt Eliza, a hapless plaything of Confederate ghosts!

When it had all begun, she'd felt fury and rage and wanted to hurt William and his crew in the worst possible way for their daily and nightly outrages of her body and soul!

Basically, the only times the ghosts didn't bother her was when Rita came up in the morning and helped clean her and bathe her. That's the only time she felt at all wholesome and good. Rita always brought her her nourishing breakfasts and, later, lunches and dinners to her room.

She also was the one to remind Amanda to take the vitamin and mineral pills the doctors had prescribed for her pregnancy. Whenever the prescriptions ran out, she wrote the pharmacists a special note and sent Rita to town in Richmond to the drugstore to get the prescribed supplements.

Sometimes, too, she got cravings for red, juicy, rare steak or pork tenderloin and certain fruits and vegetables and thought her baby telling her it needed whatever nutrients the foods contained.

It wasn't an old wives' tale. She did have cravings for certain foods. Once she took three glasses full of chocolate milk (the only type she'd drink, hating the regular white stuff) and a half a container of vanilla ice cream. She supposed her baby wanted all the calcium it could get. She had cravings for cheeses, especially Munster cheese and yogurt, too.

What would happen to her and the baby once it was born? She knew William didn't seem to care about the coming baby. Would the ghosts even leave her alone enough to properly nurse and care for it?

If now she was living a supernatural nightmare, what would her life be like once her baby was born? She tried not to think about it. When the ghosts left her alone for some hours a day, she napped, listened to soothing classical music on a particular radio station in her bedroom, and read her poetry books and novels.

Reading some of her favorites, the Bronte sisters, to escape the so sordid trap that daily and nightly surrounded her, she daydreamed that she was walking among the wild English moorlands dreaming of her demon love, William, like Cathy for her Heathcliff.

Despite all, did she still love the brute? She hated herself, but she knew she did. She hated herself even more when she realized that when the other ghosts raped and pawed her, she felt intense sexual pleasure too. That was so, so horrible! She had become just like Aunt Eliza! Oh, if only Aunt Lavinia could see her now! But she didn't dare tell any of her staff or call or write Delia about her awful situation.

First of all, if word somehow got out, no one would believe her and would think her delusional. Others, if they did believe her, would think she'd brought this all upon herself and was living as her Aunt Eliza so freely chose to life with her ghosts. One small ray of hope she felt was the coming baby. She keenly, intuitively felt the baby would be a boy.

Unlike before, she now knew her former boyfriend and past day-old husband, Craig, had really loved her. She now felt so awful for having used him and treated him as she'd done. But he probably hated her now, and if he did hear of this awful situation she was in, he might think she'd gotten her just deserts.

Despite the fact that the baby would be his, she didn't dare let on to him how bad the whole situation was now. Ah, what could she do?

She hadn't thought of a name yet, but as it would be Craig's baby, she might name the baby Craig Weston Junior. The way she was living now, between the forced love-making and rapings of both body and soul, one day just passed into another and one month gave way to another.

Was this to be like this the rest of what was left of her now miserable and degraded life? She hadn't heard from Delia in over a month. Delia had told her to forget the ghosts and leave the mansion one and for all, and something inside her made her say no.

She was afraid the ghosts would kill both her and Delia if she did such a thing of outright defiance! Then, as she finished her luncheon, there was a soft rapping on her bedroom door! It was Rita. She said, "Come in please," and Rita opened the door. She said, "You should dress now, missus. You have a surprise visitor."

"Who could that be? I haven't seen anyone in months!"

"It's your former husband, missus, Craig Weston!"

She felt transported with joy immediately and said, "Craig really wants to see me? And after I treated him so badly and all. Why, yes, I'll dress in my best spring dress and I'll see him at once on the porch! Tell him I'll be seeing him real soon on the front porch. But don't let him in, Rita. You and I both know by now, it could be dangerous for him if he came inside."

Rita looked at her knowingly and nodded in assent and entered Amanda's bedroom to assist her in dressing up for her visitor. Rita helped her dress into a pretty pink and white dress that was very loose and accommodating to her gravie, pregnant state.

Then, she did something she hadn't done in a long, long time, she opened the front door and went out on the porch and inhaled slowly and deeply the fresh spring air. The lilacs and mimosa-scented air from the gardens made the fresh air really delicious.

And there was Craig Weston, ruddy and handsome and healthy as she ever beheld him! She looked at him once and then ran into his strong arms. Between kissing him and his kissing her, she said, "Craig, Craig, I've missed you so! Oh, I've been such a fool! Can you ever possibly forgive me, darling?"

"Amanda, Amanda, if I hadn't forgiven you, I wouldn't be here now, would I? And your old friend and maid, Delia, has kept me quite informed about your life inside! She told me the ghosts abuse you and keep you indoors for months! And, my darling, you're heavily pregnant! You should be in the bloom of health, but you are haggard, as deathly pale as one of your ghosts, just so, so pallid! I told you long ago and so has Delia that carrying on like you have with those evil ghosts was all bad for you! Look, I've quite forgiven your indiscretion and foolishness with this ghost William and his friends! Come away with me! Leave this house behind! I've skipped a grade in college and now can take the bar and earn a good living as a corporate lawyer!"

"Oh, Craig, I do so want to leave this place and all its ghosts, but I'm afraid William and his ghost soldiers will follow us and kill you horribly in front of me! You know how violent he can be!"

"Listen, Amanda, love, our love is stronger than hate and malice and evil and haunting ghosts! Come away with me now!"

Then there was a blinding flash of light on the porch near her and Craig. And to Amanda's amazed eyes, the figure that materialized in the phosphorescent light was none other than her guide and long-ago ancestress, Lily.

My god, she thought, she hadn't seen Lily in almost a full year! Lily said to her, "Craig's right, you know. Your love together can vanquish William and his cohorts and send him where he can never bother you and yours again! After it's over, go away with Craig, marry together again and raise your baby together! Always remember, love is stronger than evil, fear, and hate. You got your strength and powers fully from me! Now use them!"

Then both Craig and Amanda and Lily saw William and his soldier companions with fury on their faces coming right for them.

All of a sudden, seeking deep within herself, Amanda felt the power she possessed. It had been there all the time, but like many abused women, she'd been too cowed and terrorized by William and the other ghosts to use it ever in her own defense. Well, now it wasn't just for her, she had now to fight for her Craig's very life!

Before William and his friends could reach her and Craig, she said loudly, "Stop!" and raised her right hand high in the air. A white shimmering mirror of spiritual illumination went up and William and his comrades smashed into it and were stopped dead in their tracks! They grimaced in hate and fury and frustration and screamed at her, "We'll kill you and this Craig slowly, tear you to bits."

"Listen to me and hear me loud and clear, you cannot penetrate my shield! In life, you rebelled against your own country, traitors! And you fought for the principle of slavery which is a vile abomination! You and your soldiers have tortured and tormented me for months! Well, hear this now! I banish you all, not back to Gettysburg, but to where you really belong! To hell itself for your arrogance and evil, this isn't just my judgment. I feel fully this is God's too for your evil and iniquity! To hell you go now!"

Then she raised her left hand up wide, and a black billowing cloud emerged from her outstretched fingers and covered William and the other ghost soldiers.

Craig and Amanda could smell sulfur and feel the heat of brimstone and William and the other ghosts wailed in despair and gnashed loudly their teeth, and the black sulfurous cloud engulfed them completely and then vanished with them inside it!

Amanda said to Lily, "Thank you, Lily, for helping me do it!"

"Remember, my little love, this power was for you all the time, use it well!"

And then Lily vanished completely too.

Amanda said to Craig, "I don't think we'll ever have to worry about William and his friends again! Let's leave, please!"

"Great, my car's in the driveway, Amanda."

Then a sharp pain came from her midsection and some water and blood from her private parts. Amanda nearly fell with the intense pain, but Craig caught her!

She said urgently, "Craig, take me to a hospital now, my water's broken!"

He held her and carried her in his arms to his blue car and drove directly to the nearest hospital! Everything happened so quickly, it was just a collage of fragmented images for both Craig and Amanda!

Within two hours or so, the doctors held the baby aloft from Amanda's loins in the delivery room, and with a slap on his bottom, the baby wailed a lusty cry!

The Next Day

The nurse came by and gently deposited the healthy newborn baby boy into Amanda's arms in her hospital bed. It was a private room, of course. Of course, Amanda's insurance was only the best.

Amanda looked at her baby closely. The baby could not possibly be Craig's; it had black, black hair and blue, blue eyes. His features already were a beautiful mix of William's and her own.

Whosever this baby was, he was beautiful and he was hers!, She kissed him tenderly all over and exposed her breast for the gurgling baby to nurse. It was so important the doctors and nurses told her for the baby to get his mother's milk for the colostrum, which would stimulate and really boost the baby's immune system.

Oh, how, how would she possibly explain this to Craig, or the world, for that matter?, The baby's father was a ghost!, How was this all possible at all?,

But she'd seen a lot of psychic powers and magic in general, and she knew now many, many things beyond human ken or reason, were indeed possible.

But would Craig accept him, the whole bizarre situation in general? It was a lot to ask a man to accept as his own another man's seed in the nest. And from a ghost he utterly hated too. Oh, well, what was to be was to be she supposed. Later on that day, toward the evening, Delia would come and visit her.

And what could she also say to Delia about all this? That, indeed, would be interesting. But she felt, whatever his paternity, this was an innocent and very beautiful little baby, and that Delia would not only accept him but love him, too, as she had always loved her.

The door opened and Craig came in. She looked up at him and she said, "Hi, Craig! Thank you a million for rescuing me from that mess at home! But, Craig, I'm sorry, but the baby, from the looks of him, couldn't possibly be yours. I think, from the looks of him, he's William's. And I'm not giving him up, Craig, even if he isn't yours. I love him already, no matter who his father is, even if it is William. Look, he's at least half me. He could be good, we could raise him to be good!"

Craig looked at the baby minutely too and gently grabbed his little hand. He smiled at her and said, "That little baby has a good, strong grip. I'll bet he could be a good baseball player someday!"

"And you'll teach him baseball and hockey?"

"And go fishing with him too. He's a really handsome little mite and healthy as all blazes!"

"And if people look and wonder, Craig?"

"I'll just say he's mine, Amanda. I'll just say he's a throwback to some handsome Confederate soldier from a long time ago."

"A long, long time ago, Craig. I love you, Craig, for this. And, later, we'll have a child together, I promise you."

"Honey," Craig said, kissing her tenderly and then kissing the smiling baby in her arms. "We already have a child together as far as I'm concerned."

A nurse then knocked and opened the door to check on Amanda and the baby, but seeing the handsome couple kissing on the patient's bed and the father fondling the baby, she decided not to interrupt.

What a darling scene! What, she thought, a darling couple, and quietly closed the door that they might enjoy their privacy together.

www.ingramcontent.com/pod-product-compliance
Lightning Source LLC
Chambersburg PA
CBHW022054050726
47591CB00002B/536